Chasing The Shaman

The Magic of Connecting with the Land

By

G. Michael Vasey

Table of Contents

Hey Mr. Shaman

What is it that you do?

The signs that you leave

What is their meaning?

Are you welcoming spring

And letting the year begin?

Pebble patterns all around

The silent drum beat

In surround sound

What is the meaning?

What is your intent?

Neighborhood shaman

Shadowy magic maker

Operating in plain site

Yet no one notices your

Pebbles and tobacco

No one questions

What it is you do

Except me

And I'm curious

You see

Hey Mr. Shaman, What is that you are doing?

"Try connecting with the land," she said to me.

After 11-years of living in the Czech Republic, I still felt like an alien. Never one for languages, I can understand Czech OK, but I can barely string a sentence together to save my life. Added to that, I was now living alone, my relationship having somehow imploded on me, and it seemed to me that I was actually serving time here. I work from home and none of my clients were located in the Czech Republic or Czechia as it is now called (I do not like the word Czechia, but you have to admit it is easier to write than Czech Republic!). My sole reason to be here remains my daughter and because of her, I would never leave and, being a father is not a sentence served but a joy received. Yet, the isolation, complete cultural disconnect with the majority of Czechs, and the ache of the loss of that relationship – the one that had been so important to me – had left me washed up, sucked dry and empty.

Yes, I kept going and it wasn't as if life was bad or hard – please do not get me wrong. I was and am very grateful for a job I enjoy that has me working with people all around the world and a set of hobbies like writing, story collecting and music making. I kept myself busy and connected with the broader outside world. It was just that something seemed to suck at my soul in this country. It took my energy. So much so that when I finally showed up at Sue's place to *'go out and play'* for a long weekend in Albion with her and Stuart, they thought I was seriously ill. I felt like crap. I can tell you that.

Anyway, more of that weekend a bit later. Suffice to say, here I was again with Stuart and Sue and a bunch of other like-minded magical people being buffeted by gale force winds and intermittently pelted with lumps of ice and freezing rain, somewhere up on the north Yorkshire moors standing on a hump in the moor with a standing stone stuck out of it. Yes, that's the sort of stuff I like to do for fun! It was sometime that weekend that Sue said to me *"Try connecting with the land."* She meant Czechia not the boggy mess beneath our feet on the north Yorks moors. I understood and, yes, it suddenly seemed like an excellent idea!

It's one of those funny things about magic that when you do decide to engage and open your eyes, things just happen. In those times, you have to step back and wonder about the nature of life and whether its created as we go or, more like a record, we are playing the song of our life that is already laid out for us. I have to say that I prefer the latter idea because quite often, it seems like actually, I know this beautiful song already. Déjà vu!

And so there I was one evening a few months later trudging along in the cold of Brno with my daughter's dog. I'd left it a bit late, so it was well dark and biting cold. I currently rent a place below Špilberk Castle in Brno and I take great delight in walking the surrounding parkland that is essentially the hill upon which the castle sits. It is crisscrossed with gravel and paved pathways that lead up and around the peak. Forested, it has a range of different flora and fauna that constantly changes through the seasons and the pathways offer some magnificent views of the city of Brno. More of said Castle later. This evening, I was walking at the level of my street on one of the gravel paths that leads to a stairway down to Úvoz – the street below mine. The path opens out into a large triangular space with seats and is surrounded by trees. A perfect place to engage in activities that should never be seen by the public.

As I entered the triangular space, my eyes caught sight of a rucksack. At first I thought someone must have left it there by mistake and so I started towards it. As I got closer though I realized it was open and filled with what appeared to be stones and sticks, and bones. I recoiled a bit and that is when I saw what I thought was a skeletal figure laid down by the bag. Made of stones, sticks and bones, the skeletal figure shocked me and sent a chill down my neck. Even Rocky, my cocky and well spoiled, small, Prague Ratter, jumped. I looked around to see who was the author of this skeletal arrangement but saw nothing or no one. Yet my interest was aroused. What was it? What was its purpose? I sensed that magic was afoot. I also felt like an intruder and with respect for the practioner, I stepped back and examined the arrangement from afar while ensuring Rocky didn't pee in the vicinity of the skeleton.

At some point, my interest was overcome by a sense of fear. What was this? Had I stumbled onto something dark and nefarious? I immediately took a few small steps to protect myself and, surrounded now in my mind by some nice glowing and hopefully protective light, I pulled on the dog leash to leave. Rocky also seemed to have taken steps to protect himself and was also keen to leave pulling me off into the pathway. It was then that I saw a dark figure jogging towards us. Where he come from I could not tell but he didn't give me a feeling of wishing me well. So much so that I grasped the keys in my pocket pushing one through my fingers just in case self-defense was required. Instead, he jogged past me as if I and Rocky were not there and as he passed I heard his mumblings almost as if he were talking to himself. Being alone in the dark with a madman who was talking to himself after finding what looked like a symbolic skeleton was enough for me and I pulled Rocky and set off apace.

Despite that, as I put distance between me and the man, I started to feel the curiosity come back. What was he doing? So, I took a different route to that planned and within a couple of minutes I was passing along my street a couple of meters above his position with a partial view through the trees. I stood, in awe watching the man. He had a little drum thingy in one hand which he held close to his head while thumping a beat on it and was chanting to it. I could not make out what he was saying but noted he was engaged in a little dance as well. A shaman! I had stumbled on a shaman and was now watching something of a ritual. I wanted to watch more but he looked up and straight at me without missing a beat or a word. Somehow the fact he knew I was there made me feel afraid. I had no idea what he was up to. A skeleton? Was he raising the dead? Was one thought that raced through my mind. Once again, I tugged on the dog leash and started for home. Once home, I immediately regretted that once again fear had overwhelmed curiosity. Yet, the fear was still with me. He had seen me. Might he be angry? Did who know who I was? All of these and other questions raced through my mind and I ended up sleeping fitfully and with many deep and dark dreams.

The next day, I re-visited the spot I had seen the man the night before. Me and Rocky together. The skeleton was gone along with the rucksack and I felt a surge of disappointment. But an inspection of the broader area revealed several clues. First of all, there was a large gray rock in the grass and on it was the end of a cigar. By the rock was a burned patch of grass and the burned remains of some flowers – stalks one end and petals the other. They were dark red roses and these and some other flowers remained. To me, they looked as if they came from a cemetery. Close to that was a shiny small black pebble. I had kicked it accidentally as I walked but there could be no doubt that it had been placed in a deliberately hammered location so that it wouldn't move. I carefully returned it with my foot. Rocky and I set off on the rest of our walk. I had lots to think about. What was he doing? Why had he burned flowers? And a host of similar questions.

Another thing I noticed right away were the Crows. There were tens, if not hundreds, of Crows around the spot. I had never seen so many of these big black birds around the Castle. The Crows remained through the following weeks. For several days, I had a strange feeling that I had stumbled on something best not seen. But what had I actually seen?

Figure 1: The Shaman's Mark

The Summer of Knowing

It had taken a long time to arrange for some reason. It was just a trip to the UK to spend time with friends. Well, I say friends but, in fact, I had really only met Sue once one evening in London a few years prior with my business partner and one of my sons in tow. Stuart I had never met, and I had only heard of him via Sue and the magical school they helped run together with Steve. But it was something I had to do, and I knew that I would find something of what I needed there with them. Why had it taken so long to arrange? Well, you know sometimes you put things off until the last minute and this was one of those times. I wanted to go but something always conspired to stop me, or I felt I could not. These barriers in retrospect were arbitrary and of my own making but they seemed real enough to me as I faced them. Finally though, I had made the arrangements and made the commitment. Yet, still I felt guilty going.

As I waited for the Ryanair flight at the small airport in Brno – there really is just the one flight a day from Brno to anywhere most days – I sensed a rising excitement. I was going home – just for a long weekend but still. I was going home. Would it still feel like home? Additionally, I was going to see Sue and Stuart and together, we were going to follow their birds. Sue and Stuart had written a number of books documenting their connections with the land – of Albion – the first of which they had called 'The Initiate[1].' Their magical explorations of the spiritual and physical realms of Albion had started with observing how the birds seemed to be leading them onward. Not just any bird mind, no, these birds were Kites. The idea for the weekend was to roughly follow the action in the book – the path the Kites had chosen for them. Yeah – I know…. It sounds ridiculous but that's how magic works – trust me – there will be many more examples in this book. Things happen. It is that simple.

It soon became obvious that the Ryanair flight was a little delayed. Well, no matter, I'd just have to be patient a little while longer. The delay become longer and longer, and I soon realized that my trip to the village where Sue lived was becoming threatened. It might be too late to get the

---

See Bibliography

trains. I texted to let her know. Finally, we took off and I sat looking out the window trying to calculate arrival times and so on. I was staying in a pub in the village and had no idea what time they would close and whether I could get there by then.

On arrival at the gate, we waited another fifteen precious minutes for someone inside the airport to open the door to let us in and then finally, I was through the everlong crowds at the UK border and on my way to London on the train. What with one thing and another, it began to seem to me as if I were not supposed to make it at all. I texted again to report progress. I may just make it, but it will be close, I reported.

At Liverpool St., I needed to take a tube to another railway station to get a train out to Sue's village – well actually a town nearby. By now, Sue had called the pub and they had said they would close by midnight. The race was on, but it seemed like the tube wasn't. It was broken. At some point, I had this feeling of total desperation – it really wasn't meant to be. None the less, eventually the tube started, and I was at the station looking for the last train and managing to jump on it. I then searched for another hotel online and actually called and booked one. Then my phone rang, and it was the landlord at the pub – he would stay open until 12:45 am for me. I called the other hotel and cancelled. Things were looking up maybe.

On arrival at the town, I needed to find a taxi. Of course, the two taxis at the station were booked and all I saw were red tail lights. I was then pointed into town to a taxi rank and set off but there were no taxis there either. It was almost midnight and once again it looked like I would not make it. Then, another person arrived at the taxi rank and kindly called me a cab and ten minutes later, I am in the back of a minivan bouncing along in the dark en route to Sue's village. I called the pub. I might just make it I said. I did.

Afterwards, I realized that I had originally planned the trip to arrive the following day. Then, I added a day and planned to arrive the night before. It was Sue and Stu who reminded me of this later. In retrospect, it seemed as if my arrival the day before was simply not being allowed by the powers that be. My arrival at around 1am meant that I had been made to stick somewhat to the original plan. There had been magic at work.

The next morning, I set out for Sue's home just a short walk from the Pub stuffed full of bacon, eggs and toast. As I walked I felt this huge surge of guilt for actually taking some time out just for me. And then I arrived, and Stuart answers the door as Sue was at work. I had never met him, but we were soon sat in a small kitchen talking like long lost buddies. By the time Sue arrived, I felt like I had known him for years. They were shocked by my appearance apparently and thought I was unwell. I was – I was sick in my soul and had no energy.

It's a strange thing but energy is important. The energy of places – home, work, country – these can affect a person positively or negatively. I now also suppose that how we engage with the energy of a place can have much more of an impact. I was on home soil. I was on the magical isle of Albion and I do think that my natural energy was synchronized with the energy of England at birth. Under normal circumstances of a quick business trip to London or a short weekend with my family, there was some benefit but as I was to discover, by actually engaging with the land, this energy was magnified many times over and it filled my almost empty vessel to overflowing that weekend. There is a lot to be said for Feng Shui let me tell you!

What followed was the perfect weekend. A trip by car across a part of England filled with nonstop conversation. The first stop, the rainbow chapel and its energies[2], wall paintings and the Kites. A sandwich lunch in a Templar church graveyard where a presence made itself known to us and may even have shown up in a photograph of the place that Sue took at the time. Ciders, England world cup games, and beautiful weather and conversation into the small hours. Friendship, honesty and openness. The next day, we visited a darker place – the Hellfire Caves[3] – and discussed the energies there which left us with a headache. The third day, we went off to

---

[2] See The Initiate - Bibliography
[3] http://www.hellfirecaves.co.uk/

Uffington[4] to search for the blow stone and to try our luck at making it sound, followed by a search for a dragon and a white horse before spending the afternoon at Wayland's Smithy[5]. Each step along the way seemed to be punctuated by magic – the little coincidences or strange happenings that just take place when people gather with a certain attitude of mind and spirit.

Looking back, I didn't get the message. I thought I was getting it, but I wasn't. On the other hand, that weekend probably saved me and was certainly the turning point at the bottom of a deep dive into something quite dark. I saw glimpses of light. What really also struck me was how damned personal it all was. For example, it took us a while to find Wayland's Smithy. It isn't a place that is obvious or well-marked. Sue and Stuart had been there several times before, yet they were not quite sure of the way. When we finally walked into this magnificent place, I felt... well, home actually. There is a power there and the Earth energies are very strong. The stones take on shapes and faces even as you watch morphing from one face to another and back again. The light has a strange quality passing as it does through a canopy of lofty trees. Even the sounds of birds and trees swaying seem to conjure an atmosphere and well, safety. An air of magic hangs over the place like a deep pool of soothing water. It has that quality. I lay there in the Sun and swear I might never leave. I talked to one of the stones. Confided in it my hurt, pain, confusion and asked for a sign that all might be well again and that I could survive in the Czech Republic without having the life sucked out of me.

As I stood with one hand on the stone and my eyes closed, I heard voices. We had been alone much of the time we had been there except on arrival when we had waited for a party to leave, we sat and ate lunch. Now as I talked silently in my mind to the stone and the sprits of the place, I heard voices. Opening my eyes I saw some people approaching from the path and I heard what I though was Czech. As they came closer, I realized it was Czech – not another Slavic language but really Czech. I couldn't help myself and I greeted them in Czech. The woman approached me, and

---

[4] https://en.wikipedia.org/wiki/Uffington_White_Horse
[5] https://en.wikipedia.org/wiki/Wayland%27s_Smithy

we spoke a little Czech and the switched to English. She was visiting from close by Brno it seemed. I had my answer.

Now some of you may wonder how this could be magical at all. Let me elaborate. Imagine a place far of the beaten track and pretty much deserted. Over a four hour stay, maybe six other people strolled in and out of the place. Then imagine that a party approaches this place just as you complete a monologue with a stone and two of them actually come from the very place you have come from too. What exactly are the chances of that? I could tell you more and make the odds even smaller, but some things said between me and the Wayland's Smithy stone must remain a secret.

After a small ritual peacefully conducted, we left and began our walk back to the car and the trek back to Sue's village for one last evening of company before I flew back. But there was to be another sign – another coincidence – to ensure I got the message.

Each evening, we had sat in Sue's kitchen with salad, bread and wine and talked and laughed our way through the evening. We had planned on the same for this final night, but it was getting a bit late and we would need to shop so, I suggested that perhaps we pick a restaurant and stop for dinner en route. I actually have no idea where it was we stopped – a roadside restaurant with a large outdoor seating area as the weather was glorious. We took our seats and opened the menus. And there it was – me, on the menu. Gary pizza, Gary salad, Gary and chips….. We all laughed. It summed up that one way or another, it had been the weekend that I started a recovery. The little rituals, a lot of the conversation, much of the agenda….. True friends.

THE PORTOBELLO [GF] [VE]
Sweet potato chilli hash, grilled beef tomato
baked beans, Gary baked portobello
mushroom, kale & pumpkin seed pesto,
chopped avocado, toasted sourdough
Add two poached free-range eggs [GF] [V] £1.50
Add Hash Browns [GF] [VE] £2.00

Figure 2: On the Menu (Photo - Sue
Vincent)

15

Dark Side of the Moon

The moon is a beautiful thing. I never tire of seeing it. I remember once reading about the moon and being fascinated to discover the link between it and 'woman'. The monthly cycle, the link to the tide and the association of the sea – the great bitter ocean. The dark side of the moon that is never seen was something I also now associated with the female human and at that time, not in a positive way. It seemed Madame Moon had surprised me in life as she was reflected in the woman that I had made my life. I now sought the clarity of the solar disk. The Sun shone its light on everything, and its heat gave life and sustenance. The great duality in the sky – Sun and Moon. The latter reflecting the light of the other which hid much of herself almost the entire month. Again, I thought of a certain someone. I am an Aquarian by Sun sign – bold, bright and inquiring – or at least I ought to be.

It was at the stone at Waylands that I asked where is Asteroth? The inner female, perhaps my very soul, my emotional body, or perhaps just an inner contact, Asteroth had for many years guided me in voice and vision[6]. She had shown me the way. But I had discarded her for another woman and Asteroth had been more or less forgotten. That weekend, I had a hint of her, a sniff of her perfume, a swish of her skirts, a moment of her laughter echoed again within my soul. Was she gone? Was she gone for good? For the first time in a decade or more, I felt her on the edge of my perception. On the edge of my reality. A new moon?

My return to Brno was straight forward with no delays or frustrations. As I sat back in my flat miles away from Albion, Sue and Stuart, I knew Asteroth was with me again and then wouldn't you know it, there was the most amazing and unusual thunderstorm. The weather – it always seems part of the magic.

---

[6] Inner Journeys: Explorations of the Soul, G. Michael Vasey – see Bibliography

That night, I delved into my old notes. The last record of Asteroth was back in 2006 just months before I had moved to Brno. I read my type written diary from that day. *'There was a name,'* I wrote – *'sounded like Barbarella.'* A tear dropped on the page as I read that realizing that the woman I had met, given up a life and moved continents for, was named Gabriela.

As Sue wrote me that night *"It was indeed special. By the time you had both gone, it was one of those moments when you feel 'virtue has gone out of you'. We were 'working'...all three of us...and with us, something 'other'. We just trust and work with whatever it is...and see where it leads :)"*

Meeting On A Train

Now for another bit of magic that sort of belongs to that weekend in England at least before we move on with the story. A few weeks previously, I had attended a conference in Budapest. I took the train rather than drive the 300 odd kilometers. For a couple of years, I had been more or less single and any women I had met had proven to be more damaged than I. I had concluded that perhaps that my life was now, in my late 50's, about my young daughter rather than me so imagine my surprise to find myself talking animatedly to a woman on the train and even asking for her phone number with a suggestion that perhaps she could show me around Budapest since it was her home town.

Well, I didn't hear from her. I wasn't surprised. Why would I? So, I decided to head home a day early and as I boarded my train, my phone dinged and there she was…. Apologizing for being busy and hoping Budapest had been kind to me. I replied and settled back to the trip. A couple of weeks went by and I found myself watching the first England game of the world cup alone with a bottle of wine. The phone dinged again, and it was her…. Was I watching the game? Yes, I said. We then watched the game together virtually.

A couple of weeks later, she joined me virtually for my weekend – particularly the football games – which Stuart and I could not ignore….. So there I was. Asteroth back and a new woman virtually in my life – not Czech, but not far away either and….. she was at least interested in magic a little bit too.

The Magic Continues

Whenever I have had magical experiences, it is as Sue described above. Although energized and excited by what had happened, it soon fades and takes on a dreamlike quality – you find yourself asking was that real? I was high as a kite for a week or so and little signs kept on popping up but then I took my daughter on holiday to Greece for a week while the virtual relationship at a distance continued apace. With so much going on in the day world, the other will just fade back into the background if you let it and trust me, we always do. Its calls are subtle and if you miss them, well, you just miss them. Its calls can be little signs but if you are not open to them, you simply don't see them.

Looking back though, the powers that be having just re-entered my life and woke me up a bit anyway were not going to let me slip back into the oblivion again so easily. By example I give you one night in Brno when I had agreed to meet a younger friend – Ondra. I had arranged to meet him in Freedom Square where a wine event was going on – or was it beer? I do not recall. It was alcohol and the Czech's love their alcohol. When I met him, Ondra was very happy and excited. He had been walking to meet me and passed a shop selling nuts and sweets, the girl inside had waved to him and puzzled, he had gone in to see if he knew her. It seemed he didn't but shortly would be getting to know her as she told him she was free at 9pm. *"Do you mind?"* He asked me. Who could possibly mind?

At 8:55pm, off he went to collect her and just after 9 he appeared with her in tow. For the next 60 minutes, I am watching two people fall in love or perhaps lust, right in front of me, but at no time am I unwelcome. I then notice she is wearing a hexagram and of course, I comment on it (Sue and I wrote the Mystical Hexagram[7] together). The next thing I know, this 23-year old that I just met is telling me things like. *"I think we have to live in the moment and be open to anything..... you should stop looking to find yourself, Gary and just be open to who you are..... you found him already but the harder you look, the harder it becomes to know you found him already...."* Was I

---

[7] See Bibliography

then still on the menu? Was I to be diced and fried this time or was it another pizza? Meanwhile, my virtual Hungarian friend had been telling me for 6-weeks already *"It's all about spontaneous moments – it's the only way to live."*

As usual, I wrote to Sue letting her know that the powers that be were still giving me a good, hard prod in the abdomen. She replied – *"Last night, I was writing a post about seeking... and almost used the overused quote from Rumi... what you are seeking has already found you....Sounds like the universe is taking you in hand."* I think it really was.

Later that same week, I was invited to a BBQ by a South African friend. Almost everyone there was South African, and it was a really good feast in their tradition. I met a bunch of new people and reacquainted myself with the couple hosting the party. Jan, the host, said to me quite abruptly *"You are an ar*tist." I wasn't quite sure which way to take this comment after all, I had my 5th whisky and soda in hand and perhaps he was referring to my semi-inebriated state? As the conversation progressed it became transparent that he meant I was a different type of artist. My hackles went down. What he meant by the word *'artist'* though was quite intriguing to me. He described how every time he met me, my view of the world, filled him with astonishment. *"You see the world differently,"* he continued. *"Your music, books, poems and so on are all about how you see the world. It's very inspiring, but like all artists, no one will ever understand your world view. They will just view you as different, eccentric perhaps."*

Much to our combined amazement, we were then joined by his wife who, having no prior knowledge of our conversation, immediately started to tell me exactly the same thing. Husband looked at wife with one eyebrow raised and then at me *"Gary, there is no collusion between us – this is just confirmation for you"*, he laughed.

Later, I had time to reflect on this at some length. And, I came to the conclusion, they are exactly correct! I am an artist in that sort of definition. And, suddenly, everything made sense to me. It's why I somehow never seem to find commonality with people around me – except a special few of which more later. I am different. It is that simple. And, you know what? I do not care! In fact, from now on I'm going to celebrate that I am an artist. Different. Eccentric.

The word fits me like a glove and once I got comfortable with wearing said glove, I understood that I have spent much of my life trying to fit in with everyone else. Wondering why some people would rather talk about the last night out drinking and dancing while I wanted to do was talk about why are we here? It explained this inner urge to throw words at paper to express what I feel when others are out dancing at the night club. It explained why I'm busy writing songs while others listen to the radio. It explained why I write about the paranormal, strangeness, esoteric things, magic and the other worlds of existence while others are focused on how they can escape this one.

"People want to put you in a box with others where they can be comfortable with you," my friend had said, "but, you can't live in that box – it will cause you misery. You need to say very politely to people that don't get you – take a hike! I don't care."

This conversation set me free. I realized I am the Fool, a magician, an artist. I take things into my world view with intense emotions and spit it back out in any creative manner I am able. The result always has multiple meanings clear to only a few or maybe just me. It doesn't matter. I create. I make my magic.

There are many people like me in this world. That have a different view of the world. Those who truly believe in magic and the ability to fly without wings. I know a few of them and I fit right in. The thing I now notice about these people is that they are comfortable with who they are – as odd as the world may think them. They are comfortable in their skins and defy being boxed in. After that weekend, me too.

Be who you are. Not who you think you should be. Let the real you out and sod the world. Make some magic.

I am an island

Set in an azure sea

I am beautiful

A kaleidoscope of colors

Filled with glowing light

Fertile and abundant

I am a rock

A standing stone

Timeless, eternally free

I am faces

Smiling in the Sun

Morphing shadows of fun

I am One

And also a multitude

A crowd of aspects

Moving in harmony

The many personas

Bound together willingly

I am me

In touch with identity

I am real and free

Blowing in the wind

Shining in the moonlight

Finally free

I am an artist

Seeing the world clearly

But in my own way

Pursuing my creativity

In any way I chose

This is simply me

I am Fool

Traveling the experience

Learning as I go

And sharing

Whatever I feel I know

Foolishly

Of Castles....

Towards the end of the summer, I had another chance to join Sue and Stuart in England. This time, along with a number of others on a Silent Eye[8] weekend ran by Steve. The weekend did have even greater special meaning as it was Sue's birthday. I arrived at the scheduled time and skipped through immigration without issues. I found my hotel and had an early night after all, it would be a long drive the next morning. Now, the drive from Stansted to Seahouses on the north-east coast of England looked doable. Google maps told me it would take 5 hours and if I factored in a couple of breaks, I should arrive on time around 4pm. I forgot about British traffic and more importantly – the endless roadworks – but, I duly arrived at the meeting place just 30 minutes late. Before I even got the hotel door, Sue and Stu emerged to greet me – they had been watching out for me.

This was just the third time I had met Sue – a very good friend of the last umpteen years. She and I have been through a few things and used email, telephone and thought messages to communicate. She had even put up with a call in the past months during which I managed somehow to consume quite a lot of gin to the point that when I awoke the next morning I did feel quite worse for wear and somewhat embarrassed…. Stu, I had met only that one time before and we had got on like a house on fire.

After a cup of tea – I skipped the scone and immediately regretted that – we headed for the beach where Steve gave us some thoughts while pointing out the magnificent Bamburgh Castle. There was some discussion of how on a previous Silent Eye weekend, it had rained, and everyone got wet. Sure enough, it rained, and we all got wet – I suspected this was a part of the induction process after all. As I told Sue, I didn't mind except that was my only pair of Jeans. Sue plainly couldn't care less as walking back, she waded through the thrashing post-squall waves while we all admired the light and took photographs. The Sun after the squall. It seemed an apt start somehow.

---

[8] https://www.silenteye.co.uk

A bit later, the party re-assembled in a fish and chip shop, still wet but in good spirits and I polished off a rather large haddock, mushy peas and chips. Surely, I had died and gone to heaven? Especially, since Steve suggested we wash this down with a pint at the nearby pub. I had a great time. The location was marvelous. The weather perfect. The company magical. It was a weekend spent meditating on myself as a castle – thinking about the walls I have built over the course of my life (and why I had done so) and I guess my thought was just how intimidating a castle can seem to one who has never had the pleasure of sitting before its warm hearth (heart?).

Some special moments for me included the visit to Lindisfarne (a first), having birds feed from our hands there, as well as the windy, song-ridden (seals apparently) farewells, discovering that I and another party member were born on the same date, but a different year (now isn't that a strange coincidence?), meeting Steve and the others for the first time proper, spending time talking mysteries, myths and stone circles with Sue and Stuart – as well as sinking a glass or two, and realizing that I'm not so strange – there are at least five other people like me.

The weekend was full of little magical moments, but the three of us took some time on the Sunday morning to make some magic visiting a small stone circle on the moors just below the border with Scotland. The Duddo Five Stones[9] sit atop a small hill and are reached after a hike across the countryside. The stones are always visible as you approach them and somehow they seem to get smaller as you get closer to them. On arrival, we had a bit of a good look around examining each of the stones. It is amazing what you can see in those stones with a bit of imagination – a constantly shifting scene of faces and images.

---

[9] https://en.wikipedia.org/wiki/Duddo_Five_Stones

Figure 3: The Stones

The three of us made a small ritual at the stones that morning and after we had completed it, you could feel that the stones appreciated it. It's a strange thing to say but its true. The atmosphere and the energies shifted a bit. As I examined one stone, a woman stepped around the stone, her loose clothing whipping in the wind and she smiled at me as she faded to nothingness. *"There is someone here,"* I remarked almost absentmindedly and both Sue and Stu looked back along the path we had trod to see who it might be before realizing. I have the sight. Always have had and it used to scare me now honestly I feel it's a bit of a gift. The stones and the spirits of the stones were well pleased. After a bit more time spent in amongst the stones in silent contemplation, we had to leave. We had an appointment with the rest of the party at Lindisfarne.

Now, this was September and the weather was a bit mixed. As I recall the morning was sunny if breezy. As we walked back, we reached a small copse and much to our amazement, the trees were full of butterflies fluttering around in the sun and sheltered from the wind in a natural dip. Again, here was a little bit of magic. Almost a sort of gift to us of beauty and activity given by the spirits of the stones.

Czech Despair

The rest of that Fall and winter was taken up with more mundane matters. Try as I might to get back to the UK, it wasn't to be. The girl from Hungary had become an alternating weekend fixture and the other weekend was taken up by my daughter. The months passed. Good intentions to undertake the Silent Eye course fell by the wayside as life sort of returned to a normal plod. A sort of sleep. All my life this pattern of long periods of mundane life punctuated by short periods of magic has been the pattern. Perhaps I have wasted these periods or perhaps, life needs to be lived and the path of the hearth fire calls.

The first part of 2019 was essentially the same. I made plans though to buy an apartment in Brno and grew closer to Tünde, my Hungarian. The Czech Republic was beginning to drag me down a bit again as well and in our emails, the talk between Sue and I was of bouts of bronchitis and other illnesses rather than the magical. Asteroth was somewhere there though just out of sight waiting I suppose, if these things wait for us at all. Another Silent Eye weekend was planned for September and I discussed attending saying, "*I feel like a rudderless ship at the mo... a bit of a clue from them upstairs would be nice but I think I just need to focus on discipline.*" Sue's reply suggested that perhaps I wasn't the only one feeling like that as she told me, "*I know the feeling... Stu and I had been marking time for a while, but one good adventure with the stones has set things moving again.*"

It's a funny thing but that '*one good adventure with the stones has set things moving again...*" resonated. However, as September got closer, events conspired once again to keep me from attending and by the 1st of the month, Sue was asking if I could '*come out and play*' and I reluctantly had to say I could not, but the December weekend might be viable.

The reports of the weekend after filled me with regret. Sue's account on her blog and in an email to me were intriguing and I remarked back that, "*Sounds a bit unnerving... weird. I will never forget the lady coming around from the stones last year..... an ancient woman she was ... and the trees with the butterflies.... Well - I should have come but the timing was so bad - as I will explain*

in Whitby. I really need to come and spend some time with you both. I'm drained. High BP issues....
I am sure it's the negative energy of the people here ..... I will be in London a couple of weeks so I
can grab some energy then, but I am looking forward to Whitby. The summer seemed a long dry
period somehow - not sure how to explain - sort of confused period really.... I think I'm starting to
find my way again though... we will see. How is your health? All good I do hope?"

I had had a strange turn – one of a number over the last few years since my split with Gabriela and ended up in the emergency room with what was in the end just a panic attack. Investigation into the panic attack showed up what they thought might be high blood pressure and they tried to put me on medications, but after trying three different ones and having horrendous side effects with each, I told them I would rather try natural methods. Strangely, I had managed to quit a lifelong smoking habit that January and so I was a bit puzzled by the onset of high blood pressure. I finally insisted that I felt my blood pressure was normal, but it seemed to spike when stressed either by the presence of doctors or a strange pain in my back. A 24-hour, blood pressure monitoring showed my assessment to be correct – it was normal, except when sitting with the doctor when it was sky high! The problem it seemed was my posture and sitting at a desk all day for 35-years. My Osteopath explained how it worked. For me however, I was even more convinced that this country and me just didn't get along – it was killing me and robbing me of my energy.

Perhaps I should digress just a little and talk about the Czech Republic and the Czechs. It is a beautiful country it really is. There are more castles than I can count and some of them look like real fairytale places. Each town has many places to visit – not just Prague. On the other hand, it is a landlocked nation with not an ocean in sight and for a man with Viking blood in his veins from Yorkshire, this is a serious issue. I need the Sea.

It is the people here that sometimes seem to drain me as much as I think of it being the land itself. Plainly, this is a sweeping generalization, but there are Czechs who will agree with me on this. They are the most self-centered of people, deeply envious and jealous of anyone ever

28

getting ahead either in reality or imagination. The rules for a Czech apply only to others. They are not to be applied to them. Corruption is rife even at the level of the individual cheating blatantly on taxes, or their partner, or both. Many have an unhealthy relationship with alcohol and when the beer is excellent and cheaper than water who could be surprised? Czechs constantly found ways to amaze me with their focus on themselves over family, friends and everyone else. Now, having got that off my chest, I know many exceptions who will identify the same issues in their countrymen and blame communism for this issue. The truth is that even now a good percentage of the ordinary Czechs welcome orders from above, cheap ale and steady employment without having to think too much and are deeply suspicious of anyone who would like to travel overseas as, well, as foreigners. Yes, I know. It sounds like a tremendous hit at my adopted country folk.

In 2006, when I first arrived, there were few foreigners and other than Czech, Russian and German were mostly spoken in Brno. English speakers were hard to find. How things have changed! Now, I hear English everywhere and many Czechs, especially the younger ones, speak it fluently. In those first weeks, I did meet an Englishman in a pub, and we got to talking. He had arrived right after the fall of communism and had many stories to tell. He had even written a book about it and handed me a copy to read[10]. He was headed home. "*I gave up trying to understand these people,*" he told me over his 12th or so beer.

Later, I read his book. I recall telling Gabriela that I thought it was a pile of nonsense and very anti-Czech. I even wrote a fairly damning review on Amazon. He talked about how his initial love of the place was gradually poisoned by the Czech attitude until he could take it no more. The final straw was when he took it upon himself to buy the local pub to save it. He turned it into a restaurant and hotel employing many people he knew in the village. He described how at first people were happy to have their pub saved even if by a foreigner and then how those same tongues started to tell tales of where he got his money and had an outright dislike of the fact that he was doing well. Even his friends of 20-years not only turned against him but stole money from the till. Eventually, disheartened and disillusioned he sold the business and returned to Blighty

---

[10] See Bibliography

full of negative comments about the Czech psyche. Trust me, by 2019, I had a new appreciation for his book, and I felt like I should revisit my review.

So by now, you will probably have a better feel for why I said I felt like I was having the life sucked out of me both by the land and by the people. Even though my relationship with my ex was amicable, there was also a huge sense of disbelief at what had taken place. I won't go into all of that as it is way too personal and also – there are two sides to every story, and I would not be able to balance things properly. Besides which, we get along just fine now and there is no need to rock the boat. Let's just say that I am someone who gives everything to those around him and feels guilty giving to himself. If there has been a message to me in my life it has been about this giving because slowly, it can turn into a sort of abuse. One gives, the other takes and then expects and then demands. And in an increasing need to keep the other happy, they continue to give. When I say abuse, let me be responsible and say, it is as much personal abuse as it is any other form.

I did feel sort of trapped in that I wanted to be there for my daughter for many reasons yet that meant living here. Tünde, a Hungarian and the opposite of Czech in every way was also a breath of fresh air and sanity in my life but again, I couldn't spend that much time with her either as she lived 300 km away. So my decision to buy an apartment in Brno – a new build – was an important milestone. It meant that despite everything, I was probably staying here into my old age and perhaps to the end.

The combination of this decision and the developing relationship with Tünde seemed to help me look for the magic again. My dream life is extremely active, and I have many weird dreams, but in October, I had a very strange dream indeed. In the dream, I woke up one morning and could read the metadata associated with everything that I saw. I did this simply by looking at an object. The metadata then streamed into my head telling me everything I needed to know about it. This skill allowed me to have a lot of fun in my dream.

Interestingly enough, when I awoke, I could still recall a lot of the dream details including two statements that were told to me in the dream as follows;

1. You should write this as a book,
2. This is the secret to everything.

In the world of quantum mechanics, everything is energy. There is no physical reality at all. There is only energy and a conscious observer. I explored this idea in the novel, The Last Observer[11], and had some fun with it yet, the idea of metadata emerged only in this dream. In the book The Wizard of Earth Sea, by Ursula LeGuin[12], the hero, Ged, lets loose something very dark that almost kills him. It pursues him throughout his life, and he lives in great fear of it. He finally overcomes it when he learns its name. In magic we use the idea of naming something as having power over it. In the Bible, Adam gives names to everything in Creation (Genesis 2:19-20) and in a sense, Adam was the first Magician, taking his rulership over the physical world of his creation in this act of naming. In my dream, the metadata was essentially the same thing - it was the name and associated details about everything in Creation - my Creation.

I am the only person who observes the world that I see and yes, I name it the way that I do. Everyone else, sees it differently, so yes, it is my Creation just as your world is your Creation. In my world, I have never really touched anything, seen anything, heard anything, tasted anything and so on. All of these experiences occur in the brain at the quantum level. The particles that make up my body and this desk repel one another - they can never touch. In fact, I am a cloud of particles in a larger cloud of particles and guess what? All of those particles are energy waves, and many are entangled - i.e. intimately connected whatever the distance between them in time and space. There is no time. There is no space. There is just me. Consciousness. I am.

---

[11] See Bibliography
[12] See Bibliography

"Imagination is the engine room of creation, Stan. What we imagine, if it is done with intensity and clarity, has its own reality, and that reality is the blueprint behind this reality" - **The Last Observer**.[13]

That blueprint is the thing that contained metadata in my dream. By being able to read this, I was able to make true magic. I was able to manipulate my world at will. Imagine that - the ability to truly create your reality!

I came to think of my dream as a sort of explanation of what has been called the Astral by many. The framework of energy - imaginatively fashioned and called into reality by a consciousness. It is Yesod at the base of the hexagram - one of the 7 stars of power that shows how to create reality that I discussed with Sue Vincent in our book - **The Mystical Hexagram**.[14] In the world of Yesod, the Astral light, we can read the Akasha - the metadata - and make magic.

Last weekend, I went for a day out with a Czech friend Jan. We visited Templštejn and the River Jihlava valley about 50 km outside of Brno. It is now one of my favorite places as you will see later. As we walked through the forest under a blue sky and bright sun, it was impossible not to feel the magic. I talked of this as we walked. Told him some of the same stories I am telling you and as sometimes happens, it is as if something takes over my tongue and words pop out from somewhere else altogether. *"Magic is all around us Jan, if we just focus our attention with intention, you will begin to see how as we are all part of one thing, we can connect with the land and make magic."* As I said this, a large stone suddenly rolled down the slope from above and stopped behind me and in front of him. Without even turning I said *"See!"* Of course, we stopped and examined everything, but he could see no reason for this stone to have ever moved or if there were some reason, why it had moved at that moment. Magic.

---

[13] See Bibliography
[14] See Bibliography

I have cried enough tears for you
And yet still I wish you well
And hope to see you escape your hell
It must be hard to live consumed by self
Always defensively aggressive
Seeing enemies in your friends
Holding people to a standard
You didn't set yourself

I have cried enough tears for you
And yet I still have hope
That you might finally see
You are your own worst enemy
And you are sowing your own misery
Rejecting those that love you
And chasing those that never will
As anger seethes within

I have cried enough tears for you
The loss of what may have been
That aches so deep inside
But I'm so tired of this ride
I'm tired of what I see inside
of you driving your behavior
People never change, it's said
Destiny, such as it is, is inbred

Whitby Abbey

The first week of December and I made it to the final Silent Eye weekend of the year; again run by Steve, in and around Whitby. This was great as it allowed me to visit my family in Beverley as well. Again, the weekend was filled with those little bits of magic that can convince you that magic exists. Seeing Sue and Stuart again was wonderful and lots of conversation took place about their work connecting with the land and the series of books they were writing about that work. Some of the places we visited held examples that they were keen to share with me knowing my interest. Sometimes though, what seems magical to me may not to you as it depends upon context and is often subtle. Yet, there were many examples that weekend.

The last time I had visited Whitby Abbey I was a boy. I recall little of it. Just that I was bored. Of course, I have been to Whitby many times since, often with my father who had business there. He would leave me for an hour or so to wander and once I recall taking my oil paints to paint the harbor. I was last there just a few years ago with my parents, ex-partner and daughter. I do like Whitby!

I must say that the abbey ruins are fairly impressive, but I felt no atmosphere or energies. It seemed a dead ruin to me. A stark reminder of other times. As we pondered aspects of the Abbey in the context of the spiritual prompts of the weekend, my sense was of the skeletal remains of something erected to the glory of man rather than the glory of God. What was left reminded me of what Asteroth has called the *'horny matter of experience'* – essentially, the structure that we build through life to protect ourselves, shut out the inner and act out our public outer selves. The spiritual activities that took place in the Abbey are no more and, for me anyway, have left no energy ripple in time that I could pick up on. In considering this analogy, I was reminded of how we act out roles, how we often have our sensitivities dulled by our experiences in life, and how we often lose sight of the true spiritual nature of self.

"Let go!" someone said….. echoing Asteroth again.

We had each selected four words as we set out on the weekend. As we sat eating lunch, we each first held and then fished about in a bag for pieces of paper with four words. Mine was quite a shock at first – *Meanness, Avarice, Non-attachment and Omniscience* – it said. Strangely, or rather just like me, my focus was on the negative words and not on the positive ones. I don't believe I am either mean or avaricious. In fact, I am anything but (although maybe I am blind to it?). Except, as Sue pointed out giving me pause for thought, possibly I am mean to myself.

So, as I considered this skeletal structure of the Abbey originally built to glorify God and as a place for men and women to worship and carry out God's will, I could not help but see me reflected in it. Non-attachment was the word I wanted as I considered this.

A ruined Abbey. Is this a parallel for each of us as we live life? Born perfect and innocent yet, somehow soiled through living? Erecting our defenses consciously and subconsciously around us as horny matter or in this instance, bricks and mortar, losing sight of the living indwelling God within? Some forms of religious belief would have us soiled with original sin anyway – incapable of redemption without intervention. Perhaps, however, does the intervention actually need to come from within?

"Let go!"

"Just let go…."

The contrast between the stark remains of the Abbey and **the vibrant pulsating heartbeat of the Church at Lastingham** (see below) couldn't be more apt. For me, one was a stark reminder of how life sucks you in. The other, held the promise of life….. a living, guiding inner spirit.

"Let go…."

Yes – non-attachment was the phrase of that weekend for me.

Each of us had chosen our words at the beginning. Divine providence had ensured we picked the words that would guide us and have us ask the right inner questions. I am not privy to what inner experiences the others had, but I'm fairly sure they were also profound. So much of the mystical is deeply personal and yet, also universal.

"Let go"

Another small incident of pure magic took place in a coffee shop where the six of us had stopped for refreshment in Whitby. From where I sat, I could see a bunch of books on a books shelf and after squinting across at one, I realized that it has an interesting title and mentioned it to Sue who retrieved it, opened a page at random and read. You could have heard a pin drop as well listened amazed at how relevant a random page in a random book could be! Again, magic happens but noticing it and taking note of it is another matter altogether.

The penultimate stop of the weekend was the church in Lastingham and a visit to its beautiful crypt. The remains of St. Cedd are supposed to be buried just to the right of the alter under the small church and there are a number of old carved stones to view. On approaching the church, I could feel it. Energy!

Once inside the church, I could feel it pulsating strongly and I remarked to one of my colleagues – *it's like a heartbeat*! Down inside the crypt, the heartbeat was strong and regular. To sit there and silently experience the energy pulsating was I think possibly the highlight of the weekend – along with the Sticky Toffee Pudding with masses of custard I had experienced the evening before....or perhaps the dance of the Foxes in Whitby.

These weekends often have many highlights and magical – WOW moments that I genuinely believe are magical that spontaneously happen when a group of like-minded souls get together. Back to that energy though. The heartbeat from inside the Church. It is Earth energy but possibly at a point where water enables it. Water is represented by the downward pointing triangle in the Hexagram – as is Earth. Earth represents groundedness, stability, potential, and stillness, while water can represent birth, fertility, and refreshment – as well as washing, cleansing and baptism. As I sat in the crypt in silent meditation, feeling that pulsating energy, I did feel grounded finally and cleansed.

It was a truly magical moment that was experienced alone and yet in the company of my weekend friends. Each of us experienced the energy in our different ways and each of us took something very special away from that church...

After the weekend was officially over and we had said our goodbyes, I followed Sue and Stuart onto a couple of other stops. One was a church that they had visited multiple times but never been able to get inside as it was always locked. After parking the cars, we made our way up the path to the church door. Sue tried it. Nothing. Stuart tried it. There was a feeling of resignation – it was closed and locked again. *"Let Gary have a try,"* Sue said finally. I was a bit despondent to be honest. The door was plainly locked. Why would it be different for me? But it was. I twisted the knob and the door opened. We all looked at each other with a sort of shrug of the shoulders that said – magic happens!

A final stop was made to show me the wall paintings in Pickering. We spent many minutes examining these amazing images in reverent silence. Then, it was time once again to part. But there was time for one last small ritual outside of the church. The three of us made the ritual using the water Sue had collected at the final stop outside of Lastingham when we found the Mary Magdalene well and all filled small containers that Steve had thoughtfully provided for exactly that moment. As we returned to the cars to say our goodbyes, Sue repeated something to me that she had said earlier in the weekend....*"Try connecting with the land,"* she said. *"Stuart and I have often wondered if you have a karmic connection to the Czech Republic or maybe a past life thing going on. Try connecting to the land and see what happens. You know how to do it."*

Hunting Dragons

Since this book is about magic, it would be remiss of me not to say again that magic happens and if you are open and observe, you will notice it. Some people talk of coincidences – strange events with even stranger timing – me? I call that magic. And so in the sadness of parting with friends and yet in the clarity of that different level of consciousness you experience in a weekend of magic and contemplation, I made a vow to myself, to Stuart and Sue and to Asteroth, I would connect with the land. In fact, I think it is true to say, I could not wait to do so.

Travelling back, it struck me that in all the time I had spent in Brno – some 12 years – I had never really tried to look at the land in the same way that I did the UK. England was the land of Arthur and his knights, Ireland was the land of the fae, Scotland, Wales and Cornwall the lands of the Celtic myth and legend. The UK was the place of stone circles and of magic through to the very beginnings of human time. It resonated with spirit and had a detectable soul. It was this that Sue and Stuart had been exploring and connecting with for several years and it was this that they had shared with me and others via the Silent Eye and their books. I could feel the energy. I could experience the magic. I could remember the past and the history.

To me, by contrast, the Czech Republic was simply where I needed to be. I had searched once for stone circles and found little. I had given up so easily. Yet, if the truth be told, there was something about Český Ráj (Czech paradise) and its sandstone turrets, forests and castles that had captured my imagination. There was something about the natural and nature in the Czech Republic that did in fact resonate with my soul. I had simply never really listened to that nor given it much importance. The Czech Republic was also the place that a magician who had fascinated me for decades was born, lived and died in František Bardon and it did have a rich tradition of magic and magicians. I had just never really acknowledged that. The closest I had come was to write a book about the paranormal in the Czech Republic that had taken a huge detour into myth and legend. Or was it?

On my return, I went through my blog and realized that in fact, I had perhaps at times started to connect with the land. For example, there was this,

"Over the last few years, I have increasingly enjoyed getting into nature. I am also rekindling my interest in geology and these days enjoy nothing better than getting out into the wild with my hammer. There is a magic about certain places that I have noticed more and more recently. You can sense the nature spirits and of course, the Goddess herself in such places..............Even in the recent past, I have experienced strange mystical experiences walking alone in the bosom of the Goddess. You can feel the energy. You can sense the magic and power of places like streams, waterfalls, exposed hilltops and deep in the forest. Increasingly, I have found that I want to photograph and capture some of that beauty and I am presenting a few such images in this article.

To me, this beauty and vibrancy is something we must keep on reminding ourselves of. It is too easy to become lost and barren in our concrete jungles of cities connected by fibers of light hidden underground and glued to our computer screens. I am reminded of an article I wrote a couple of years ago (see below) about symbols. In that article I said that 'Reality is a set of symbols to be observed, contemplated and learned from..' The most important symbols are those we often take for granted and provided by Mother Nature like rain or an icy day. I think we must observe and look. We must try to spot the symbols and contemplate what they might mean to us as individuals. These symbols are hidden in plain sight all around us. All you have to do is lift your head and look - often in nature."

And this,

"I read recently somewhere on the internet that inner contacts can be viewed simply as symbols. I apologize to whoever wrote this as I cannot recall where I read it and who wrote it, but it was a bit of a critique of the concept of inner contacts altogether! But the thought has persisted with me.

Standing outside just now puffing on a cigarette, I noticed a mall patch of moss. It was bright green and truly beautiful. As I noticed the moss I started to look around and observe. The

trees, the blue sky, the birds singing. *The amazing beauty of nature. All symbols. Life is a moving movie of symbols that we simply need to observe and puzzle out their meaning. That bright green moss, that little island of emerald greenness shimmering in the sunlight reflecting from the dew that had settled there. What did that mean to me? It reminded me to look. To observe and to marvel.*

Asteroth too is a symbol. It is a symbol that speaks to me of inner truths and yes, beauty too. She is the archetypal Goddess, the inner me. She has shown me other symbols including the hexagram and helped me observe this symbol in many different ways – many planes of reflection – some of which are described in the book The Mystical Hexagram. But she has also pointed to other symbols – even created them in my inner reality awakening something magical and something delicate. Places with spiritual purposes for quiet contemplation.

Reality is a set of symbols to be observed, contemplated and learned from and if we miss an important symbol then it keeps arising in our consciousness until we notice. Perhaps this is the synchronicity that occurs to people where some symbol repeatedly occurs in our lives. It's our inner selves' way of saying – look, observe, contemplate and accept."

And as I revisited these articles now forgotten, I noticed another thing – another little piece of magic. Both had been commented on at my blog. By Sue. Her comment on the latter article was,

"This is a beautiful piece of writing, my friend, as much for the imagery as the concept it describes. We are all guilty of living asleep to the possibilities and beauty of the life around us, most of the time. Every so often we awaken and see the world anew, as if the clouds had parted letting in a fleeting ray of sunlight."

I also found this,

"I commented somewhere recently – I am in a Goddess phase – and I really am. She is on my mind – I even had to write a poem about it.

Today, I went down to the forest and, choosing a part of the path deep in the forest where a small stream passes, I called on Her. I lit and placed a small candle and left an offering. She was all around and everywhere.

I have periodically dreamed of Her. She is **the** beautiful woman of my dreams. She is also the deep and strange fears that I harbor deep inside. More importantly, she is the inner me – my anima. She is every woman I meet. She is the temptress, the sexy vixen, the aloof and haughty woman, she is the mother figure, the daughter, the grandmother, the cold, evil calculating bitch, the kind neighbor, the partner. Each of these is showing an aspect of the Divine Female and reflecting back something of my own inner make up.

It's almost a full moon tonight. She hangs in the sky Her powers growing and her monthly cycle almost at its peak. The wind is howling at the top of our hill here in Prague. I can feel Her power."

The poem I had written was this one called The Ache,

This inner longing
It rises sharply
curling, winding, unbending
Seeking, I know not what
Snakelike, uncoiling
My senses boiling
An ache so deep
A need so great
Needing, I know not what

It's in the trees
It's in the fields
Its also in the mountains
The hand emerges

41

Sword held aloft

Ripples form and spread

It's everywhere I turn

But can't be reached

It's all around me

The fires burn and burn

Flickering, twisting

Rising upwards and on

I'm lost in bliss

Sensing laughter – happiness

The aching rises

Seeking, writhing

But not finding

It's release

Dear Lady, take my hand

Lead me where you will

Be my guide, my Mother

Maiden, crone

Ease this ache

Let me know I'm not alone

Somewhere

All is one

It begins

Just to End

An endless return

The eternal Breath

I am a child

I feel alone

I ache to end it

To be reconciled

Cleansed, to rest

Hugged, caressed

One – with the Goddess

Needless to say, Sue had commented on this too. Then lastly, I recalled a day in Prague and searched my blog for this,

"Today, as I descended into the valley behind our flat and started along the tree-lined mud pathway, I sensed something. For some reason, I invoked the Goddess. Loudly and verbally. I asked the Goddess and the nature spirits of the valley to be with me and to help me in certain things. It just seemed so beautiful with the autumn leaf colors from yellow, through greens and browns to red. The sunlight sparkling in sheer rays through the treetops. The gentle bubbling of water running down the small brook to the bottom of the valley. I was content.

But then, it happened. At first, I thought it must have somehow started to rain as I heard what seemed like raindrops hitting the leaves of the trees all around me but instead of rain, leaves fell. The leaves swirled around and around as they fell down all around me like a snowfall of multicolored leaves. The gentle sounds I heard were leaf hitting leaf and it sounded like rain. At the same time, my other senses suddenly became more alert and I could feel an energy in the vicinity. The back of my neck tingled, and I relaxed into that warm energy. The leaf rain moved, and I followed it. I marveled that this leaf rain was only in a single location and it moved along the pathway.

I mean I checked all around. There were no masses of leaves falling from trees, no breeze rustling the treetops and disrupting the leaves there. I stood watching and began to laugh.

43

This was surely a sign. My involuntary invocation had been heard and a nature spirit or perhaps even the Goddess herself playfully revealed herself to me. What a gift.

Even as I walked out of the forest and back up onto the road, the leaf rain seemed to follow. Not only that but I became aware at one point of a small finch-like bird singing and eyeing me. Even as I passed not a foot underneath where it was sat it did not move. I held my breath as I passed and turned as I walked to watch it in song. I stayed a while and still it sang and watched me until I felt it was time to move on.

As we reached the crest of the valley, my dog ran ahead a little and out of the bushes arose a huge bird. Not more than 10 feet away I watched stunned as a huge bird of prey took off and flew over my head and out over the valley. I have no idea what type of bird it was, but I have never seen such a bird here before.

Even now, I am wondering and in awe of this experience. Amazing and a reminder to me that the Goddess is all around us if we will but look."

In those moments, I felt a rush of excitement as I knew that Sue and Stuart were absolutely right. There was a connection here and it needed, had to be, explored. Me being me, that very night, I googled and googled and googled. I was a man on a mission, and I was looking for search terms I had never tried before. I wanted to connect with the land, with the Goddess, with Asteroth in a new way... and if you know me, you will know I am not to be put off. I used my blog again that night to record my plans and to record something of what I had discovered,

*"In following the activities of Sue Vincent and Stuart France across the landscapes of the UK – start with **The Initiate**[15], which is a great read and will give you an idea of what they are up to – I was also pointed by Sue to the author Paul Broadhurst and just completed his book on*

---

[15] See Bibliography

the Green Man[16]. Having read that book, I now also get a bit more of what Sue and Stu are onto in the UK and having just come back from a weekend of magic with them and others in Whitby, it got me to thinking...... what about here? Here being Brno in the Czech Republic. Well, the first thing that struck me is that Brno is symbolized in part by a dragon. The dragon hangs in the old town hall in public view in fact. There are lots of stories about the dragon – which is actually a crocodile including this one[17],

"that a Dragon made Brno his home and threatened the citizens and all of its livestock. Merchants stopped coming to the city to sell, and women stopped going to the market. The plan to kill the dragon was thought up long before somebody with the courage to actually do it came along or before a master plan was thought up.

Luckily, one day a butcher who was traveling through Brno volunteered. So the courageous butcher created a trap to get rid of the Dragon. The trap was a sack made of fur (ox or sheep) and filled with lime. The dragon became very thirsty after eating this fur and lime, and after drinking so much water at the river his stomach expanded with the lime inside, and it burst! Then, the citizens celebrated by having the dragon preserved and now we can see it hanging from the Old Town Hall – and you might notice, this dragon looks a lot like a crocodile."

There are other stories about how Brno ended up with a stuffed crocodile and a dragon story but whatever the truth, the crocodile dates back to the late 1500's it seems at least! Some of the local sport teams are called the Dragons and the city has made the dragon one of its images.....

And then, I started to discover other dragon myths in the surrounding countryside. Like this one[18] (translated by Google),

---

[16] See Bibliography
[17] https://blog.foreigners.cz/brno-tales-and-legends/
[18] https://www.blanensko.cz/o-loupeznikovi-a-drakovi/

"Once upon a time, two horrible brooms plagued the region. So terrible that the rumor of it has been preserved up to our times.

A terrible dragon settled in the county and attacked and frightened the whole village. There was no one to defend himself, bravely oppose the monster. So the dragon raged furiously at will. Destroyed, gagged, killed. Woe to a man or an animal, woe to a farm or a village when suddenly the ominous dragon's wings murmured over them.

No one in the neighborhood knew where this four-legged monster had its lair. Indeed, no one dared search for it. According to the direction of the dragon's arrival and departure, it was judged that the monster was somewhere in a vast rock maze in the grooves of the Punkva Valley. These conjectures were not far from the truth. The dragon chose the inaccessible bottom of the great Macocha Abyss as his home. There he set up his lair in a spacious and dry cave. While hunting and spoiling during the day, he flew to Macosh for a night's rest, to whose dizzying deep bottom he could safely endure thanks to his mighty wings. He could rest in the abyss in complete peace, and the Macos' lakes provided him with good, cool water.
The second and no less terrible scourge of the region was a large bunch of bandits. The troop, led by the skillful and ruthless lap of the Obeslik, became a terror and horror of human lives and property within a short time.

He had his scouts everywhere, so he couldn't miss anything in the wide region. The burghers, the villagers, and especially the rich merchants, kept complaining to the Margrave's authorities. They begged for help and asked for a criminal expedition against a bandit. But the gargoyle skillfully escaped justice for a long time and hurt hilariously.

When the near surroundings of Brno were no longer safe in front of Obesik and his pawns, the Margrave himself went against the bandits with a large section of the arms people. And then the last hour of the gang struck! The robber company was first carefully monitored, her stay in the woods tracked down, and finally gripped by such a tight circle of pursuers that there was no more escape from him.

The puddle knew it was all over now and gave up. The captured robbers were hung on the spot, Obesik was drafted in handcuffs to Brno castle. There he was brought to justice and tried for his countless crimes.

Over the malevolent robber Obeslik, a pest of land and property, was sentenced to a far more cruel and terrible judgment than the loss of the gate. "You shall be set aside, the chief of the band of robbers, the bandit, and the great masters; Only a loaf of black bread will be given to you on a journey that will not return for you."

On the third day after the sentence, the paw was chained, loaded on a chariot, and taken to Macosh for justice to be done. When the armed parade with the convict arrived in Vilémovice, in the vicinity of which the Macocha Abyss is spread, the armor-bearers took the robber out of the wagon and tied him along the forest paths to the abyss. The horror and horror conceived of the Fiddler that he was trembling all over his body when, after reading the judgment, he was tied with a rope around his chest, brought to the very edge of the depression and slowly lowered into the abyss.

How awfully horrible the view was to the bottom of the great abyss! The hard-hearted bandit, who was not afraid to spend a few human lives at times, almost fainted as he glanced over the steep walls of the abyss. Macocha opened her hell-throat as if to devour the unfortunate. He hung on the rope between the sky and the earth for a long time before his feet touched the solid ground at the bottom. A loaf of black bread was lowered behind the robber. When he milked him, he would starve!

The ropes were pulled up and all the noise stopped. The loner was lonely in the gates of the gruesome underground empire. There was a dead silence, only the raging waters of Punkva *that appear at the bottom of Macocha, then disappearing into the mysterious hatches of countless holes, and the glory disturbing the calmness of this wilderness that perhaps no human foot has yet entered. The robber glanced around the wild abyss, where two lakes were gleaming in the gloom of the dying day, and he knew he couldn't help him, and he would starve in a few days.*

The ghost of night fell slowly into the landscape as suddenly high above Macocha's esophagus something tremendous flew over. Lapka lifted his head and stood. A huge monster was slowly coming down to the bottom of the abyss. The horrified Obeskin had barely enough time to hide in a small cave, from where he watched with a stunned breath the circling of a terrible dragon who sat in the bottom of the abyss in a short while. The dragon monster went to the pond first and joined it well. Then she slowly crawled down the loam to the large cave where she had her lair. It wasn't long before Macocha's hoarse echoed. The dragon fell asleep.

The bandit relaxed unwittingly. The monster did not seem to notice him. So he was saved so far. The cave provided him with a good and dry shelter, and thus, overwhelmed by fatigue and everything he had lived through this day, he was not far from sleep either.

As the morning dawned a little in the abyss, the dragon woke up. But Obesik was already awake and in good hiding, hiding behind a large boulder, was watching the dragon's actions closely. The monster stretched lazily for a moment, spreading its hideous, bat wings as if it were about to take off. Then she rocked down to the small straight at the lakes, waved her wings several times, and circled the Macocha space in large arches until she flipped over the edge and disappeared in an unfamiliar direction.

The precipice was calm now, so the robber could think and think about everything. He was aware that getting out of the bottom of Macocha without help from others was impossible. If only he had the dragon's wings! And that just brought him to a saving idea. What if he sat on the dragon's back? Only then could he get out of the abyss and save himself from death. Yes, only the dragon can help!

He couldn't wait for the evening, so he waited impatiently for the monster. It was very dark when he heard the familiar whisper of wings. The dragon was returning. The monster flew back to the pond to quench its thirst. Then she crawled into her rocky lair, from which she would soon snore again. The puddle had a plan, but he almost lost all the courage at the sight of the monster. In the end, however, he carefully climbed the scales of the wings to her back and gripped tightly between the wings.

Sleeping dragon, lucky for Obešlíka noticed nothing. Just in the morning with several powerful booms of massive wings, he lifted the bottom of the abyss up and with it the robber Obešlík, desperately holding the scales between his wings. Soon the edge of the abyss flew over, and the dragon headed for noon. Now the waiter waited for the right moment. When the dragon descended close to the ground, he slid off his back and fell, as a miracle without injury, into the tall, forest grass. He was saved. He had just lost the hair of certain death by hunger at the bottom of the great abyss. At the same time, however, he did not want to figure out what would have happened to him if the dragon had observed him.

The gargoyle was saved and also at large. But he still had to earn and secure this dearly acquired freedom. He watched well in which direction the dragon was leaving Macocha, where it was heading. It was on this basis that he based his plan. If he had been able to kill the dragon, he would certainly have been instrumental in not only the security of the entire region, which had been so freed from the gruesome scourge, but had also washed away its earlier offenses, which even when he was on the verge regretted.

He did not miss long and went to Brno. He reported to the margrave himself and told him extensively about what had happened to him and around him since he'd been dropped into the Macocha Abyss. But not only that! He volunteered to try to kill the dragon monster if he *was forgiven for the acts he had committed during his robbery life. The surprised Margrave finally agreed. However, the puddle asked for three things: a live calf, a spear, and quicklime.*

The brave bandit got what he demanded and left Brno Castle to prepare for a decisive match with the dragon near the Macocha Abyss. First, he sharpened his spear. Then he killed the calf, ejected his viscera, and filled his belly with quicklime. Then he sewed the skin again. When he was ready, he carefully followed the dragon's flight from Macocha, searching for a place where the monster was resting, searching for a stream or a forest spring to drink in a wide circle around the abyss. And happiness pleased him. A faint hour from Macocha he found a well at which he found numerous dragon claw prints. I decided to take a bold attack at this point. First, he brought the calf killed and laid it near the well. Then he chose a safe place in a nearby grove, where he could see the well and where he was well hidden from the dragon. And he waited patiently.

Shortly after noon he heard the miserable rustle of wings, and the horrible beast was already plunging into the meadow by the well. But she barely stood on solid ground, showing some unease. She looked around suspiciously and turned her head to where the dead calf lay. Immediately, she threw herself eagerly at the sudden prey, opened and closed her terrible jaws several times, and the fat bite disappeared into the voracious mouth. And then the dragon only did what the courageous Obes kid expected. The thirsty thirst drove the dragon to the well to drink a fat lunch. The dragon drank a little while this time when he started to scream. The water began to work in his stomach, filled with quicklime. The monster swept from side to side, rolling in terrible pain. Her belly swelled to rupture.

The obesee, watching closely, decided that his moment had come. He stepped out of hiding with his spear in his hand and headed straight for the dragon to hit him with the last blow. A spear whistled through the air, and a well-guided wound cursed the dragon's belly. He just grunted and suddenly it was over.

Due to the courage and bravery of the former robber, the vast region was deprived of tribulation. By doing so, Obesik had atoned for the nasty acts he had once committed. He was now not only forgiven and free, but also richly rewarded for his heroic deed.

This dragon lived in the Macocha abyss in the area known as the Moravian Karst – an area of limestone and, of course, caves close by Brno, and then suddenly, I found tale after tale of dragons in the area around Brno……

Dragons, it seems, are often associated with areas of Earth energy and ley lines. It is thought that perhaps the bad dragons with noxious breath, might be references to areas where the earth energy is negative or has somehow gone toxic if, for example, the energy has been cut off. It would then need a knight in shining armor – perhaps a templar – to use a lance of light or perhaps the mirror of his armor to rectify the situation and put the dragon to rights – restore the earth energy to its rightful place.

A week ago, I drove through a place close to Brno called Dolní Kounice. I had never been there before. My 12-year old daughter was with me and she remarked as we entered the town that she felt nervous and didn't want to stay. I felt it too – it was the wonderous pulsation of the Earth energies and I vowed to go back to explore further. A quick google showed me a couple of things. Firstly, the village/town has an annual dragon flying event for kids (kites) and other 'dragon' events at the castle but more importantly, it has the ruins of a convent called the Rosa Coeli as well as a myriad of chapels and monuments that seem to hold promise...

The convent has many stories attached to it, but it was established in 1181 and finally abandoned after a fire in 1703 – it also has amazing energies associated with it. On the hill above the town is the chapel of St. Anthony with its annual wine pilgrimage on May 5th. I suspect a chapel in such a prominent position has a much earlier history and the whole town needs to be explored.

I wrote that day in my blog – *"So, in 2020, I will be hunting dragons in Moravia…….. it seems there are plenty to hunt."*

Yep, I was about to become a regular St. George except that I discovered that in these parts, he might be better identified as Perun.

And Templars too?

It is funny how attention works. By giving something your attention, you sort of give it power. As I had written in *The New You*[19], energy follows thought and so if I think about something and give it your attention, You energize it. In fact, I might go so far as to say that magic is merely the act of giving your attention. It could be an idea, it could be a vision of something, it could be an aspect of yourself, but whatever you chose to give attention to, you will give it energy in your life. Faith moves mountains and attention can too!

So when I arrived home, my attention was on earth energies, pagan monuments, Templar activity, and the land itself here in Brno, Moravia and the Czech Republic. I kept telling everyone and anyone the same thing *"Why had I never seen this before!?"* when discovering Templar sites a stone's throw from Brno or when discovering pagan sites even within the city – even just outside of my own window! I knew the answer – attention. My attention and focus was now on connecting with the land – finding a connection. It manifested itself in multiple ways in a sort of sequence.

In follow up emails, Sue had not only told me to do what they did (her and Stuart) but also to read a book by Paul Broadhurst and Hamish Miller called *the Sun & The Serpent*[20]. I ordered the book, but it would take weeks to arrive, so I googled it and discovered a TV program about it on YouTube. Next I was making divining rods out of coat hangers and googling for mentions of dragons in the area where dragon could be a reference to Earth energy – just like I had experienced at Lastingham in the crypt. I don't let the grass grow under my feet... when I am excited by something, I go for it and it gets my full and complete attention see. But I couldn't stop asking – Why did I never know this before? I mean, I have lived here 13-years and it never occurred to me to do this? Why? How?

---

[19] See Bibliography
[20] See Bibliography

Soon, I was organizing my own first trip to connect with the land. The search term 'Templar' had brought up a lot in relation to the Brno area – I was shocked. Imagine my surprise and delight to find that the Templars had in fact been located very close to Brno! Apparently, the Templars had entered Bohemia in 1231 during the reign of King Wenceslas 1 (Yes - the one who looked out on the feast of Stephen!), first establishing Jerusalem in Prague but by 1248, they had also established themselves in Moravia at Čekovice near Brno, and by 1250 at Jamolice, also near to Brno. How did I never know this I asked for what was probably the millionth time?

At the earliest opportunity, I was off to visit one of the sites - I chose Jamolice as it happens, and the ruins of the Templar Castle called Templstejn. Unfortunately I didn't have too much time and I was also dragging my reluctant 12-year old daughter with me, so this would just have to be a quick recce trip to prepare for a longer one in better weather (It was -1C and snowing!). As we set out and I entered the location into the GPS in my car, I realized that this site was on the banks of the River Jihlava - the same river as the ancient convent of Rosa Coeli at Dolní Kounice, which also sats on the bank of the River Jihlava - interesting huh?

Finding the place proved to be exceptionally difficult. But at a town called Ivančice, we began to follow the river going in the opposite direction to Dolní Kounice – to the south-west. We passed through several small villages as the road narrowed slowly to a single-track highway. The first village we hit was nothing special - just a bunch of small houses and farms by the side of the road and yet, to my utter amazement, one of them brazenly flew a Union Jack! In all my time in the Czech Republic, I had never seen a home flying a Union Jack on a flagpole and I wondered who, why and how they managed it? knowing how patriotic the Czechs are..... A little sign perhaps? More magic?

As we hit the next village, I had to stop and back up. We had passed a church, but this church was, well, a bit weird. Czech village churches have a look, you know - a certain style. This one looked very different. It was Romanesque. I photographed it for future reference and research. I learned that the church was dedicated to St. Peter and St. Paul and had been built in the second half of the 12th century. Its layout was considered unusual with apses added to three sides. I would learn much more on a subsequent trip.

As we followed the river further along, we came across a very recent monument built in local stone and wood to the Templars called U Tří Templářů. The monument had been opened only very recently on a cycle path. The land above it and to the side of it had that look - as if it has at some time past been worked by humans. We spent a few minutes examining the site with an image of Baphomet, two templars and a throne.

Then we set off again down the roadway by the river but eventually had to stop as we entered a gorge and the track seemed to become impassable for a car. Despite my pleas that we should get out and walk further, my daughter was having none of it and so reluctantly, I gave up on my pursuit of Templštejn for another day. Next time, I would bring proper walking gear as I could see that a hike was going to be involved as the place is not accessible by road - at least not if you still value your vehicle. Besides, the walk would be very interesting. So, we turned away and headed back the way we had come. Yet as usual fate had another sign for us. The old car that we followed down the road back to Brno actually had a red Templar cross sticker on it!

A promising start but the holidays were to afford me another opportunity on Boxing Day. Tünde and I took a trip to revisit Dolní Kounice. It was a beautiful, but very cold day. When we arrived, we soon discovered that the Convent was closed unfortunately at this time of year and it would not be open it seemed until April, which was not unexpected, but a tad disappointing. The Convent ruins are remarkably intact, and you can pretty much walk around the outside of it - which is what we did - detecting some energies in one direction that I would hope to investigate further another day.

The convent stands under the castle and by the shore of the Jihlava river and an old mill. With the Convent being closed, we walked leisurely through the village and towards the white chapel of St. Anthony, which sits on a hilltop on the other side of the river that had caught my attention last time I had been. The route up to the top is marked by the stations of the cross and as we reached the marked footpath to the top of the hill, the first station of the cross emerged in somebody's back yard!

Figure 4: Rosa Coeli and St. Anthony's Chapel

After a while, the climb became quite steep and windy with gusts of a cold wind howling across the hill. Periodically, there was another station of the cross to examine and on reaching the top, we were rewarded by stunning views of the town, the river valley and Rosa Coeli convent below as well as an ice storm!

The chapel on the hill was locked but it is a rather recent building it seems, dating from around 1750. The original wooden chapel dated back just another 100 years according to information on the site. It is only opened for the annual pilgrimage in June. I suspect an older presence on that hill, but so far, I cannot find any documented evidence of it.

Figure 5: Rainbow

The hilltop is a beautiful peaceful place high above the hub-hub of the town below and I can well imagine that it has been a place of meditation and worship for many centuries. The wind truly whipped around us with intermittent rain and sleet even though the skies were blue in some areas. I had a feeling that the afternoon was one for rainbows and we kept looking to see if we could see any - facing away from the sun. However, it wasn't until we had descended the hill and walked back to the car that we were rewarded with a magnificent vision of a full double rainbow over the hilltop chapel. Somehow, I had expected this - seeing it in my mind's eye when still on the hilltop - and, I took it as a sign that the afternoon was well spent.

Once home, I set about a bit of research online and discovered that the Chapel of St. Antony was built originally in 1654 as a wooden building and then replaced by a brick building a century later. As stated in the Deeds of Foundation of 30 April 1654, its construction was initiated by the Lower-Bohemian citizens in honor of the patrons of St. Antony and St. Florian "*to intercede for the people who suffer from various fires and floods every year.*" The Stations of the Cross were built later, sometime in the early 19th century. Apparently, a pilgrimage to St. Anthony' Chapel takes place every year in June.

The Rosa Coeli Convent was planned as early as 1181 (and the site was chosen in such a way that it would remain hidden from those coming from the South Moravian plain) in the river's bend to the south of a hill where a huge castle was later situated. Two years later, the monastery was built. It was most likely originally just the convent and an oratory built from wood and the stone buildings were probably started much later. Extensive remains of a (another) Romanesque stone church have been preserved in the outer masonry of the western and northern cloisters.

In October 1183, it was occupied by nuns from the Louňovice monastery in Bohemia. In the 14th century it was rebuilt, and the Romanesque basilica was replaced by a much larger Gothic church, with a new cloister in the north. After the death of the Provost Count John VI from Althan in 1517, a certain Fr. Martin Göschel took over and he was apparently an ambitious priest who later converted to the Lutheran faith and even took one of the nuns as his wife. This caused some consternation as you might imagine, and the Bishop of Olomouc and King Louis of Jagiellon issued an expulsion order against him, but Göschel ignored it and remained in the monastery until 1526. He didn't end well though as he was imprisoned, interrogated and tortured, and only saved from being burned alive by the intercession of some nobles, who instead put him in prison where he finally died. Meanwhile, the other nuns chose a new provost, but the scandalous life Göschel had led in the monastery resulted in the locals indignantly assaulting the monastery. Although the buildings were maintained, a fire in 1703 resulted in significant damage. Despite gradual repairs, the Convent fell into disrepair.

Today, the many visitors to the Convent ruins often talk of the energy in the place and it was that that attracted me to it. Unfortunately, as of writing, the place remains closed due to COVID-19 lockdowns and I have been unable to explore its interior. I have though walked around it with my divining rods and detected energy lines that run through it and across the town. There is more to be learned about the place, but it will need to wait for better times.

A month or so later, Tünde and I were again able to explore and this time, we chose to revisit the area around Templštejn. The first stop was back at that strange church - St. Peter and St. Paul's in Řeznovice. Arriving, I was again struck by how different the church is to the average church in the region. Excitedly, I rushed up to the door only to be disappointed by the fact it was locked. This has certainly been a feature of Sue and Stuart's work in the UK where they sometimes seem to be barred from entry of a certain church and so I was resigned to the fact that probably, we were out of luck, but at least we could look around the outside. Suddenly though, a woman's head popped around the back of the church and said "*Je to otevřene*" (It is open!). It seems the entrance was actually around the corner!

Figure 6: The Templar Church

Once inside, I began an exploration of the church. Czech churches generally are usually fairly modern inside having been rebuilt at some point in the recent past post-communism and some work had taken place here - so no green men or that kind of thing peering at you unfortunately, but plenty of mystery. To be honest, I did not detect any unusual energies in the church, but it was certainly intriguing. The visit was a little rushed as the woman was cleaning and preparing the church for a service. A man was vacuuming while she was preparing the seating. I was told the church would be closed when they were done, and I asked for *'5 minutes'*. They smiled and said, *'no problem.'* The church must be visited a lot as when I signed the visitor's book, we skimmed through the many entries from people from all around the world.

The church is really very different and is celebrated as the only example of a Romanesque church in Moravia although there are a couple of other examples in and around Prague. Part of the church was demolished in the 16th Century to add a new rectangular nave. The octagonal tower formation, topped by a pyramid, rises above this part of the church. Strangely, the floor is thought to have been made 70 cm higher than it was originally and the church at one time was actually a two-story structure!

The church was built after the demise of a nearby hill fort known as Rokytná and the nobleman who had resided there, set up in Řeznovice instead. The church was a private chapel for this nobleman. When the nobleman's line came to an end, the buildings changed hands several times and in 1259 it belonged to the Oslavany monastery and later, probably to the Templar comanderie in Jamolice and Templštejn. After 1312, it was acquired by the Lords of Lipá, who granted it as a fief. From 1538, it belonged to the Oslavany family, was abandoned in the 30-year war and by 1784, it had become a parish church.

In the 14th Century, a religious text was written into the northern apse and paintings added around the middle of the 16th century. Some of the paintings remain and these were rediscovered in 1947 when the church was reworked and are said to be images of St. Andrew (with a diagonal cross) and John the Evangelist. Above them are half-figures of angels with nscription strips, and part of an image that belongs to a missing figure of Christ. In the lower part of the southern apse is a six-line inscription made on a stone. In one of the side altars that was demolished in 1791, it is said that evidence was found attesting to the reconsecration of the church on 26 October 1483 in honor of St. Peter, St. Paul and St. Andrew.

Figure 7: Wall Painting of St. Andrew

nside and on display, there are the tombstones of Markéta Hadburková of Žarošice (died 1584), Kateřina, daughter of Petr Ried (died 1584), and the heraldic tombstones of Hrubý stonemason Petr Ried (died 1575), and Ctibor Hostakovský of Arklebice (died 1603). There is also an nteresting stone bearing Kuman inscriptions (Kumans were a nomadic Turkish people) from the early 14th century. The inscription was apparently not deciphered until 1952 by Dr. Pavel Poucha and it is a strange font similar to Uighur and mentions a '*Marqusz*' - it is said to be the name of a Kuman warrior who died in Hungarian service. There is also another stone bearing a striking

Templar cross. Both of the latter certainly caught my attention and during later googling, threw up some interesting mysteries as follows.

Figure 9: The Templar Cross

Figure 8: The Kuman Stone

At the beginning of the 14th Century, the nearby town of Ivančice was apparently burned down the troops of Duke Albrecht I of Habsburg. His auxiliary troops were largely composed of the Kumáns, a Turkish nomadic ethnicity. The Kumáns originated from an area that gradually extended from the Black Sea to the borders of present-day Mongolia. However, Tartar and

Mongolian expansion eventually pushed them deeper into the center of Europe. Here, a certain proportion of the Kumán population found a new home in the territory of Hungary, where it subsequently adopted Christianity and became part of the Hungarian nation. Dr. Poucha deciphered the inscription on the stone as MARQUSZ, which corresponds to the Christian name Markus, or Mark. The stone may be a fragment of a tombstone of a Kumán that was buried there. However, why was the traditional script used?

The mystery deepens as on the outskirts of Ivančice, there is said to be a small hill, still called Kumán. According to legend, it is a burial mound built by the Kumáns above the grave of their late chief. The story is remarkably reminiscent of the legend of the last resting place of the legendary Atilla the Hun and a golden treasure of immense value. In the first half of the 20th century, amateur archaeological surveys were conducted here, but they did not support the theory as the base of the hill seems to be made of natural rock.

Interestingly, the name of the village, Řeznovice, is translated in German to 'Regensburg' where a similar Romanesque chapel was built. Perhaps the link is that the builders of the Regensburg church came to build this one? Some people have observed a similarity of the markings on the Kuman stone to old Germanic runes and the since the stone only has eight and a half identifiable characters, who is to say who is right? We do know that it is not a forgery, as Bohuslav Balbin in his Epitomae of 1677[21], speaks of a *"church that is paved with tombstones of the Kumans."* While he doesn't mention the exact location of the church, its general location is given as between Ivančice and Oslavany, near Brno, and must surely be this church. So, Germanic runes or Kumán text? Who knows?

Next to the Kumán stone, is a another one deeply incised with a Templar cross. The Templars first founded the commandery in nearby Jamolice and then later moved it to a more strategic headland watching over the Jihlava River - Templštejn. The ruins of the castle are also surrounded

---

[21] https://en.wikipedia.org/wiki/Bohuslav_Balb%C3%ADn

by many legends, one of which tells of a secret underground passage from there to this very church and, in some legends, to another castle near Brno many miles away. According to some sources, the grave of the last Templštejn Commander may be hidden by the church.

For me, exploring the land in this esoteric fashion often brings remarkable coincidences and events. These little magical happenings are of great importance to the person experiencing them but may seem less than magical to an outsider. On this trip, I was accompanied by my rather bemused girlfriend who, while enjoying the history and the trip, was always a bit suspicious of the underlying intent. Strange then that the first visit should be to a Czech church with a Hungarian mystery as she is Hungarian and lives in Budapest! The second little bit of magic was the connection of this remarkable church to the Templars.

A prior trip to discover Templštejn had ended with the realization that I had somehow taken a wrong direction - at least for a car - yet the end of that journey was the discovery of a beautiful gorge in the Jihlava valley - well worth seeing. As we left Řeznovice, I determined to try a different route - one that took us actually into the village of Jamolice. This was where the original Templar comanderie was set up in Moravia according to the history books, and the small village still proudly carries the memory of that in its coat of arms.

Jamolice is a small village that essentially hugs the sides of the road passing through it. Once inside the village, we saw a sign pointing ahead to Templštejn, but we drove right through the village without seeing another. I was a bit confused as I thought the entrance was in the village however, around 1km outside of Jamolice, we found a second sign and pulled off the road and parked. According to my phone GPS, we had a bit of a hike ahead and the day was cold - below zero - and windy, so we wrapped up warmly and set off - my new dowsing rods in hand. After around 2 km, the pathway began to descend gently into the forest and towards the river valley below. The wind was howling and as it ripped through the treetops. It seemed to me as if the forest sang to us a melodic song of rustling leaves and swaying boughs, and I remarked to my companion that it reminded me of the day in Prague when the Goddess seemed very present via the wind in the trees. Maybe she was talking to me again?

After a short and gentle descent, we finally saw a thick stone wall emerge from the forest. We had reached Templštejn! The peace, stillness, and quietness of the place contrasted to the howls of the wind whipping through tree tops we had experienced earlier. I thought the quiet somewhat strange actually - perhaps magical even. The first thing to see is that huge thick wall - possibly 3+m thick - made of the local Gneiss - a whiteish looking rock when weathered. Behind the wall lay the ruins of the castle complex.

Figure 10: The Templar Castle

The ruins were sold off by the Czech forestry a few years ago at auction and are now owned by a private individual who, along with volunteer groups, is slowly trying to reverse the decay at the site. It is free to visit, and you can see that some work has been done to preserve what is left of the site. He has also put up a website[22] - which features a lot of articles, news, legends and so on about the castle and though in Czech, it can be translated by Google if you set up automatic translation in the browser.

I was pretty excited to be honest and we climbed up the huge wall that we had first seen via a wooden structure erected for the purpose, but which looked a bit flimsy and care was needed to ascend and descend safely. The views from the top were magnificent looking down into the Jihlava valley and I could see the gorge where I had been with my daughter. There was also a kids camp down below – it is a tradition here for kids in the summer is to go away to camps - and this was one of those camps.

After that we walked around the ruins, exploring as best we could, and I definitely found an energy line passing through the corner of the site that I could pick up on both sides of the castle as well as inside it. I didn't feel any particular atmosphere, but the quiet was eerie. We discovered the well - which is very deep and safely covered with a sturdy steel framework to make it safe. I tossed a coin down it with a wish and it took quite a while before I heard the gentle clack of the coin hitting rock.

A brief history of the castle is as follows - The first mention of the Templars in the area is in Jamolice in 1297 and the castle at Templštejn was founded between 1281 and 1298. In 1312, the order was abolished, and the castle was bought by one Bertold Prikner who later sold it to Přibík of Šelmberk in 1349. By 1379, it was owned by the Lords of Lipá who expanded and rebuilt it. In 1482, the castle became the seat of Ososky of Doubravice, but the castle was later again taken by the Lords of Lipá. The estate was confiscated after 1620 when the Lipá heir took part in some

---

[22] http://www.templstejn.cz/en

unsuccessful uprisings and was abandoned after a fire shortly after. In reality then, the castle was only held by the Templars for a short period.

According to the official website, there are lots of interesting legends and rumors about the place including hidden treasures (in the well), tunnels, ghostly knights, and so on. The castle was probably occupied by older Templar's whose fighting days were done and who were tasked with administration of the rich estate. One interesting legend involves the old Templars being called upon to help defend the area and sending a young page instead all dressed up as one of the order. In short, when this young page arrived, his horse bolted, and he charged the battle scene inadvertently. The enemy thinking a Templar force had arrived quickly dispersed and victory was had. The page returned to the Templar fortress and was rewarded with a grant of land. No archeological work has been done apparently, but some finds are stored in a museum nearby that one day I will go and visit

Walking away from the castle, for me the sounds of the wind and birds came back as we reached the top of the valley and left the silence and peace of Templštejn until the next time.

On our return, I plotted the Castle, the church at Řeznovice and the convent Rosa Coeli at Dolní Kounice on google maps and discovered that they all lie on a straight line – perhaps a ley line? I'm not surprised, and I do think that somehow they are linked to each other in terms of their siting and original use. A future project will involve seeing if this ley is associated with energy lines.

Earth energy

The next day, we headed towards toward Mikulov on the border with Austria where in the morning, the plan was to climb 'Holy Hill.' Mikulov[23] is a beautiful town at the southern end of the Pavlov Hills and in the wine growing region there (Pálava is probably my favorite Czech wine). The town was founded sometime in the 12th Century and is today dominated by a fine Chateau at the center of the town that stands on a rocky hill called Zamecký vrch. It was originally a Romanesque castle that was rebuilt in Gothic form and then as a Renaissance chateau and is now a museum. Mikulov is also famous for having been home to the most important Jewish community in Moravia prior to World War 2, and there is a large Jewish cemetery in the town for those who wish to visit it. It is an exceptionally pretty town, and full of things to do and places to visit.

However, my objective was the hill forming the eastern boundary of Mikulov called Svatý Kopeček - or Holy Hill. I had never climbed it in all the visits I had made to the town over the years - frankly, I was too lazy to climb the 330m of Jurassic limestone! The hill is holy because it is a pilgrimage site that had 7 stations of the cross and a chapel built to thank God for saving Mikulov from the Plague by Cardinal Francis of Dietrichstein (1570-1636), Bishop of Olomouc. According to the towns' website[24], the history of the hill and the buildings on it is rather difficult to reconstruct.

The first building was probably a chapel dedicated to the protectors against the plague. Its foundation stone was consecrated on July 2, 1623 and the whole building was completed in 1630. At that time, a stations of the cross with seven chapels representing the seven passion stops were probably already built and the appearance of Holy Hill remained unchanged until the mid-18th century. In the years 1750-1776, seven more chapels were added, so that there were 14 stops. The site is also famous for the Procession of the Mikulov black Madonna. A tradition of Marian

---

[23] https://en.wikipedia.org/wiki/Mikulov
[24] http://www.mikulov.cz/turistika/pamatky-a-prohlidkove-objekty/cirkevni-pamatky/krizova-cesta-na-svaty-kopecek/

68

pilgrimages began in 1865, when the statue of the Mikulov Madonna was brought to the Holy Hill.

But there was probably another motive behind the creation of the way of the cross and the chapel on the hill. This was to use the hill, then known as Tanzburg Hill, and rename it to Holy Hill. Tanzburg Hill (Tancovat - to dance) was actually known for its long pagan history and legends say that the name originates from the dancing performed on the hill to celebrate nature and fertility. It still has a reputation for its strong Earth energies and for an ability to heal and bring fertility. Although it is hard these days to find much detail about the pagan past of the hill, it seems that it had a long history and a reputation that included witches sabbats and even a legend about a dragon and a princess! So they basically Christianized a pagan holy site. But my ears pricked up at the mention of that dragon!

As we climbed the hill, you immediately notice the white Jurassic limestone. It is hard and quite angular making it difficult to walk without sturdy shoes. Many of the stations of the cross along the way occupy recesses or small caves in this hard limestone. It's quite a climb actually, and although it was a beautiful sunny day with a blue sky and not a cloud in sight, the wind howled and froze any uncovered flesh. It also brought home strongly the idea of dragging your own cross up a hill to your death.... so it serves its purpose I suppose. Every step of the way is blessed with the most amazing views of the town and at the top, the vista is amazing.

Of course, the Chapel and the bell tower were both securely locked and inaccessible, so we were unable to look inside of them. But honestly I wasn't there for them. I got out my divining rods and started hunting for the energy center. It wasn't at the bell tower as many websites suggest but actually a bit further behind both it and the Chapel. We sat for a while taking in the peace, the energy, and the amazing views. I meditated there for a while, but then resumed my search. I soon discovered a rocky outcrop in the middle of a shallow depression on the edge of the hill. My rods crossed over the stones whichever way I approached them, and I was soon sat on the shiny surface of the rocks. I could feel the pulsating beat of the Earth's heart. It felt very similar to Lastingham.

It was then that I noticed that the stones seemed to crop out in the center of a circular depression. Was I imagining it? The back of the circle seemed to be natural outcrop, but as it turned around in front of the stones, it seemed to me there were deliberately placed rocks. The more I looked and examined with my Geologist's hat on, it seemed to me there was a circle here with the stone and center of the energy in the center of the circle. I couldn't convince my companion though.

I again meditated and engaged in some mental ritual. I was rewarded with images of swords - an image that I used to see in my late teens and early twenties and one that I physically saw on the Island of Eigg in Scotland (story is recounted in Inner Journeys: Explorations of the Soul)[25]. I was amazed and surprised by these images, which were vivid and full color. It seemed to me that the sword represented a calling of some kind - an idea I explored in meditation for a while. I then beckoned for my companion to come down from the seat she had sat on to bask in the sun and views, and to come to the center of the energies. She was a bit doubting to say the least until she too sat on that rock.

When you find this sort of a place and this sort of energy, you just never want to leave. You would be content to stay there snuggled up in Mother Earth's pulsating heartbeat forever if allowed. There is power there. I wanted to see where the energy went - I was expecting a line you see. But, starting from the stone - the center - the rods sent me in a circular motion around and out from the rocks - a sort of Fibonacci curve shape! I shared this with my companion who remains a tad skeptical of dowsing and energies in general. No matter which way I looked at it, this energy was not a line going from one pole to the other, but a vortex with a spiral shape around it. At this point, I was getting some funny looks from other folks on the Hill - it was really busy! - and so I decided to sit again and take it all in.

---

[25] See Bibliography

Eventually, we ran out of time and needed to make the descent again vowing to return. I had found what I was seeking - real Earth energies. I had connected with it, and seen images and gained guidance that would, since it is reputed to be a healing energy, give me a troubled night. I won't go into what form that took but by morning, I realized that I had faced something I had found shameful in my past, finally recognized it as an issue and started on resolving it. It was a healing. My companion told me that she had now the energy to start her week at a challenging job.

In the evening and now alone, I was able to google for information on the hill. I was particularly interested in whether my impressions of the stones as the center of the energies was correct and whether there was a circle of power there. The first thing I did was go to Google Maps in Earth mode and zero in on those rocks and there it was - a near perfect circle around the rocks just as I had seen there. I am convinced there is something there of a more ancient and pagan nature. I then stumbled upon a blog[26] of a Czech person who highlighted mineral deposits around the country and had visited the Hill in search of Calcite crystals. He had taken a pendulum and he remarked at the strong Earth energies and how his pendulum had gone crazy - not by the bell tower - but on top of a small rocky outcrop. Could it be? Yes - there was a photo there with him, pendulum, and smile sitting atop the very same rocks. Validation?

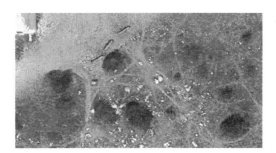

Figure 11: Google Maps Image of the Stone Circle on Holy Hill. Note the two rocks at the center of the circle – this is the vortex.

---

[26] http://www.kameny-krajina.cz/lokality/mikulov/index.html

71

After visiting Mikulov, we headed back to Brno taking a short detour to a town named Čejkovice. I wanted to take a quick look to see if there was anything there worth spending time on later. Čejkovice was the second Templar establishment in the Czech Republic after Prague, and the first in Moravia when they arrived in the 1230's. Just as in the case of Jamolice, the town's coat of arms recalls their presence.

Unfortunately, not much is recorded regarding the presence of the comanderie - only a mention in 1248 in a document issued by the Lord of Břeclav apparently. The history of the town is given by the website of the Chateau[27]. It is also the third-largest wine town in the country and sits in the center of the Moravian wine area.

The Templars built a fortress, a church (dedicated to St. Kunhuta) and a tower. The fortress eventually became the said Chateau - which is now a hotel! The Templars were also engaged in the wine business locally it seems, and a provincial Templar commander is believed to have lived there - a man by the name of Ekko. The Templars are also thought to have constructed vast wine cellars by the Castle, which are still in use today and are known as the Templarske sklepy or Templar Cellars, and tours can be booked it seems. There is also a wine maker and label that I see every time I visit the supermarket and always thought to be just a brand. It turns out, this is the Templar wine maker for real. Why had I never realized that before?

Now the interesting thing about Ekko is that he died in around 1310 in 'Resnowitz' - which is the old German name for the town of Řeznovice – the town we had started the weekend at with the unusual church. It seems that Ekko is the Templar commander buried there. In fact, it may have been his tombstone we saw on display inside the church! He was a pretty important, it seems being head of the templars in Bohemia, Moravia and Austria until 1308.

---

[27] https://www.hotelcejkovice.cz/en/history

Again, the Templars are always associated with strange legends due to the order's wealth and supposed practices. In this case, there is supposed to be a Templar treasure hidden somewhere in the vicinity of the fortress and the cellars are reputed to extend for many kilometers underground.

We pulled up to the Hotel Chateau hoping to get at least a coffee only to discover it was closed. It would open the very next day after a winter break! The cellars were also closed with no possibility of a tour until April at the earliest, while the church is now a modern building - though it may still be worth a visit. So after a short and chilly walk to take a few photos, our weekend was over, and we headed back to Brno. Strangely though, and a little more of that magic perhaps, we had come full circle and in an unexpected way. The famed Templar commander who resided at Čejkovice - our last stop - turned out to be the one buried in the church that we had started at. It seemed apt.

Mapping Earth Energies

It hadn't taken me very long at all once I had given my attention to it. I had found a Templar presence in the area as well as a Christianized pagan presence at Holy Hill in Mikulov and I believe also at the chapel on the hill in Dolní Kounice, with its stations of the cross, was likely a similar Christianized pagan site. By placing all of these sites on a map, I was able to draw more or less a straight line through them – a ley line perhaps? In the future, I will test this theory and also look to see if there are male and female energy lines crisscrossing the ley line at the important locations – it would not surprise me at all to find that to be true. Perhaps more importantly, I felt now as if I had started to tune into the energies of the land I now lived in. I was connecting to the land and now, instead of draining me, it was beginning to light me up.

Now, as I have mentioned before, I currently live close by the Špilberk castle that dominates the Brno skyline. I had taken to walking the many pathways around the castle with my daughter's dog and now I thought I should try exploring the castle area with my rods. I also discovered a really useful application for my iPhone to help me map anything I found. So, I started exploring with my 'sticks' in hand.

When I was a teen, my father had made some rods of his own. He swore by them and used them to find pipes in the yard and even wires in the walls. I recall one weekend we took them on a trip to the coast, and he and I walked around looking for water. I discovered I could use them very easily. I never forgot about those rods.

So there I was every night for weeks walking the castle paths, rods in hand seeking energy lines. I found them too and what was more startling was that I could track them into the streets and neighborhoods of Brno as well. The project is far from complete due to having to hang up my rods for a while during the lockdown, but I have mapped two lines passing through the Castle where they cross by the Castle Chapel and then extend outwards into the city.

What is really strange is that I expected these lines to be straight and so you sort of expect to find the extension in a place as a straight-line projection of the last point. I soon discovered this was not the case. I would walk up and down almost willing the rods to cross where I thought the line would be and not find anything and then 50 or 100 meters away, bang! There it was.

Figure 12: iPhone Map of Energy Lines at Spilberk (Arrow marks). The solid lines is the path I took to map.

This activity is another way that I am connecting with the land and the energies in my local area. I am giving the energies around me my attention and I think, in the process, whatever this energy is, it becomes aware of you and soon it is an interplay of energies. Just like the way that the stone circle came alive when Sue, Stuart and I made a small ritual there and I saw the spirit who smiled as if to say – thank you! Suddenly, I am yearning to be in Czech nature and when there, noticing things I might never notice like butterflies, beetles, flowers and so on.

A strange thought came to me one evening as I was thinking about mapping these energy lines. I was wondering what energy lines were? – where they came from? and so on, and suddenly a thought popped up – Wyrd. The women of Wyrd or the three Wyrd sisters spinning their web of Wyrd – what if part of that web was Earth energy and the Earth energy lines?

The ancients sensed these earth energies and used them. They built huge structures where earth energy lines seem to cross. How did they use them? Brain Bates in his novel *Way of Wyrd*[28] has the apprentice being taught how to use lines of the Wyrd web to propel himself through space. The book is fictional of course, but the thought was that perhaps the ancients knew a lot more about energy lines as a web? And maybe , they saw their fate as wrapped up in that web of energy lines. Perhaps this is the Wyrd web spun by the three sisters? Something to ponder?

[28] See Bibliography

The Slavic Gods

Until recently, I had simply been enthused by how quickly I was able to connect with the land once I had done what Sue had suggested – which was in essence, give it your attention. I was sort of content to have made such amazing progress – as I saw it anyway. I felt that as I was connecting with my adopted land, it was opening up new possibilities for me in life as well. Although Asteroth was not the in-mind entity she had once been, I knew that somewhere she was involved and on occasion she showed me little signs. I call them magic. Some call them coincidence, but put a string of coincidences together and really, what do you have? Magic! And what is magic at the end of the day? It is working upon yourself in order to have a magical influence on the outer world. It is about changing the inner self via spiritual alchemy so that you see the world differently and in doing so, create a different world. It is a virtuous circle. But I was yet to meet the Slavic Gods.

Tünde was coming to visit and although it was not yet spring, I thought it would be good to explore a bit again. In my googling, a place named Hostýn had come up many times as a place of natural energy and it was close enough to visit in a day in the car.

Svatý Hostýn, or St.Hostýn, is a hill in Moravia and it is a place of special devotion to Mary. Wikipedia says this, *"According to a traditional legend, first recorded in 1665 by the writer Bohuslav Balbín[29] in his work Diva Montis Sancti, during the disastrous raid of the "Tartars" [30] in the 13th century, people who were seeking asylum here lacked water and they prayed to Mary for help. It is said that a stream of water came out of the ground and a powerful storm forced the Tartars to retreat."* (Translated by Google)

That being what it may be, the site is also very ancient, and it was once perhaps a Celtic fortress or settlement of some kind. The first mention of Hostýn dates back to the middle of the 16th

---

[29] https://en.wikipedia.org/wiki/Bohuslav_Balb%C3%ADn

[30] https://en.wikipedia.org/wiki/Mongol_invasion_of_Europe#Invasion_into_Central_Europe

century when it was known as Hoštejn. Archaeological work confirmed that the site was far more ancient and had been a Celtic settlement around approximately two hundred years BC. There was always a natural spring at Hostýn, and this may have been part of why they chose to build a settlement on its peak – that and it was easier to defend. Moreover, it was also a safe place, the top of the hill was already surrounded by a massive protective wall. Built about 1500 years BC, the Celts allegedly deposited piles of stones, covered them with clay and then burned them. The process was repeated in several more layers. This made the stone wall quite solid. The wall is about 1825 meters long and was interrupted in places where there may have been gates. It is reportedly up to 13 meters wide and 15 meters high in some sections. Artifacts from that period including ceramics, amber jewelry, whorls from looms and even hut foundations, have been found there, and a small Celtic water reservoir has been preserved. So, the water plainly wasn't anything to do with Mary. It was always there. In fact, Wikipedia says (translated by Google),

"The first medieval chapel of Virgin Mary was probably built by the miners and was first mentioned in 1544 without any reference to the legend, which probably originated from the existence of massive walls, a chapel and spring near the hilltop. At the time when the legend was first mentioned by Bohuslav Balbín (1665), it was a clear analogy to the contemporary war with the Turks. After another successful war against Turks, there were an increasing number of pilgrims visiting Hostýn, so a new basilica was built in 1721–1748, together with Via Crucis, the pilgrims' hospice and other facilities.

Another chapel was built next to the spring of "holy water", which was believed by locals to possess a healing effect. This led to the nickname "Moravian Lourdes" for Hostýn. A 240-step stairway from the spring to the basilica was constructed in 1909.

In 1903 new open-air Stations of the Cross were built by the architect Dušan Jurkovič and are now a major tourist attraction for the region, together with the basilica itself, attracting not only Catholic pilgrims but thousands of other tourists. The largest crowds at the site were in August

1912, when the main statue of Virgin Mary was crowned by the golden crown blessed in Rome by Pius X. The number of pilgrims and other visitors was estimated to be 200,000 within ten days.

Figure 13: Hostýn Chapel

The day we visited it was really, really, windy and that wind was biting cold. It was also a Sunday, so I didn't get into the Basilica because there was a service going on. I did take my rods and I did detect an energy line going straight into the front door and passing directly through the water chapel lower down the hil, but the cold wind made my hands so cold, I didn't persist with the rods. For me, the place lacked the presence I had hoped for until I was sitting in front of the well. In fact, as is typical with many Catholic sites, it's all rather tacky and commercial with lots of small huts selling everything from plastic rosaries and crucifixes to sausages with ketchup! Despite that, the Basilica is beautiful indeed and well worthy of a future visit in warmer weather.

It was actually down the hill a bit that we found the water chapel. Dedicated to Mary, there is a real energy there that put the hair on the back of my neck on notice. It is sited on a natural spring and a variety of taps, sinks and so on allow you to take some of the water, which is clean, ice cold and nice to drink. It is said to have healing properties and I would not at all be surprised as the place is pulsating with earth energies. I collected a bottle worth while others came with plastic gallon tanks and filled them up to the top.

What puzzled me most was the way in which 'Mary and child Jesus' are depicted. 'Mary' stands afoot a large and prominent crescent moon and in the hands of the baby Jesus is a strange device from which emanates lightning. I have seen this device and lightening before - with Zeus. Also, while I was there, I had Mary Magdalene in my mind the entire time as opposed to Mary, Mother of Jesus. Plainly, this site is one associated with feminine Earth and Water energies and it is also associated with healing and miracles.

Figure 14: Mary and ?Jesus

So, as you might imagine, puzzled by the images and myths, I started to do more research. First of all, we have 'Mary' standing on the crescent moon shown really as a lunar goddess – actually something you see rather a lot in this part of the world – but then what is going on with baby

Jesus? Well, after some input from Sue and Stuart, I was led to a Slavic God named Perun. He is the God of the sky, thunder, lightning, storms, rain, law, war, fertility and oak trees in the Slavic pantheon. Having come up with that name, I googled it along with 'Hostýn' and I found myself back on the monument's website and an obscure page there where Google translated the following,

"One of the most beautiful and mythical hills in Moravia is Hostýn. It has attracted the incoming since time immemorial. The first experiments with iron were performed by people of Silesian-Platenian culture, the Celts had the largest Moravian oppidum. The Slavs also liked here, in the 12th century, Czech princes built border fortifications. The most famous story relates to the Tatar invasion, and the images and sculptures depicting this legendary event can be seen today in the Hostýn Church of Our Lady.

In the 13th century, Tatar troops stopped under Hostýn. A few months before, they had defeated the flourishing European knighthood in Poland, and now it seemed that nothing stood in their way all the way to the Atlantic. But in Hostýn, a higher power arranged something else in the form of a miraculous storm and floods, and the Tatar hordes were forced into a humiliating escape. The storytellers sing about the originator of the miracle depending who they are worshipping. The remnants of the pagans, the survivors of the peaceful Christian mission, thanked Perun, while the Catholics thanked the Virgin Mary.

Later, the Church of Our Lady was built on Hostýn (the Catholics won this dispute); a monastery, a chapel, and Stations of the Cross. A famous pilgrimage site was established here. Pilgrims attracted a number of vendors, stalls were built along the stone staircase, then the hotel. On the former Celtic acropolis towers rises, a few years ago it was overtaken by a wind power plant."

The myth of the founding of the place goes back to this supposed battle with the Tartar army and the miracle that was said to have taken place.

"In the 13th century, and this is a historical fact, the Tartars launched an attack on Moravia. The towns people took to the hills, to the site of an ancient Celtic settlement mainly because it had good defenses and a water supply. Besieged by the Tartars, the inhabitants prayed to the Virgin Mary. Their prayers were answered. A storm broke out and lighting struck the tent of the Tartar leader, killing him instantly. The invading army decided to no longer pursue the inhabitants and fled."

Back in those times, Christianization of the region had only been partially successful. While the aristocracy may well have been devout Christians, the ordinary people had a reputation for clinging to their Slavic roots and Gods. In fact, a Slavic Christian church was in existence at that time that, in effect, tried to have its cake and eat it too. As Wikipedia again states,

"Many elements of the indigenous Slavic religion were officially incorporated into Slavic Christianity, and, besides this, the worship of the Slavic gods has persisted in unofficial folk religion until modern times. The Slavs' resistance to Christianity gave rise to a "whimsical syncretism", which in Old Church Slavonic vocabulary was defined as dvoeverie, "double faith". Since the early 20th century, the Slavic folk religion has undergone an organized reinvention and reincorporation in the movement of Slavic Native Faith (Rodnovery)."

So could that solve the mystery? Could it be that in a nod to Slavic paganism, the Catholic Church had adopted an image that actually shows the Slavic God Perun as the baby Jesus? And if it had, wouldn't that simply be an extension of the "double faith" discussed in the Wikipedia article? I also find it interesting that the miracle points to a miraculous storm brought on by Perun, the God of Thunder and the skies, and the God of the Slavs – and there was weather and magic again.

So once this little mystery was unraveled, I realized that I knew nothing about the Slavic mythology nor pantheon of Gods. Again, I had to ask myself why I had never thought on this before? And once again, I found myself reading avidly about the Slavic pantheon of Gods and about the myths and legends told by the Slavic peoples in the region.

Actually, I have always adored myths and legends. Growing up, I was addicted to stories of the Greek Gods, King Arthur and other such tales. I also enjoyed fairy tales and read them avidly. My favorite was one called Rumpelstiltskin. Imagine being able to turn straw into gold? Just like an alchemist. Old Rumpelstiltskin is depicted as an Imp or Goblin-type creature, but the name is also reminiscent of the German words for a poltergeist. The girl eventually goes 'deep' into the woods where she watches him singing and he reveals his name. According to some sources, this story or a variant of it, could be up to 4,000 years old! Notice how the girl goes deep into the woods.....in order to learn the name of the Imp. Deep into meditation or a trance, and into another world? There is magic there.

Fairy tales and myths are stories brought to us through the centuries often through an oral tradition and passed from generation to generation before being collected and embellished in more recent times. They contain great wisdom and I happen to believe great that it is 'occult' wisdom. They appeal to all and provide a way and a means to pass on knowledge to each new generation.

Yet, I am not so familiar with the Slavic fairy tales and myths. Yes, I had cherry picked a few stories in my short book of Czech ghost stories[31] such as the founding myth in which three brothers are cast out of their own land find and move on to found the nations of the Czech Republic, Poland and Russia (Čech, Lech and Mech). I have watched the very many movies made locally that cover a lot of the more common fairy tales over and over again (It appears to be a Czech tradition to have these movies on TV every year at Christmas and other significant times). Yet, having lived here 14-years, I have realized that I had little knowledge of the Slavic Gods nor the myths and legends of that culture. It was time I learned a little.

It was the visit to Hostýn that caused me to realize this, and as I searched to try to explain to my own satisfaction why an image of the baby Jesus was depicted like Zeus, I reached out to Sue

---

[31] See Bibliography

Vincent and Stuart France. They pointed to a Celtic deity synonymous with Zeus and that led me to Perun, the sky God of the Slavs. In turn, this led to the tales of the duality of Perun and Veles.

"In Slavic mythology, much like in Norse and Baltic mythologies, the world was represented by a sacred tree, usually an oak, whose branches and trunk represented the living world of heavens and mortals, whilst its roots represented the underworld, i.e. the realm of the dead. Perun was the ruler of the living world, sky and earth, and was often symbolized by an eagle sitting on the top of the tallest branch of the sacred tree, from which he kept watch over the entire world.

Deep down in the roots of the tree was the place of his opponent, symbolized by a serpent or a dragon. This was Veles, watery god of the underworld, who continually provoked Perun by creeping up from the wet below up into the high and dry domain of Perun, stealing his cattle, children, or wife. Perun then pursued Veles around the earth, attacking him with his lightning bolts from the sky. Veles fled from him by transforming himself into various animals, or hiding behind trees, houses, or people; wherever a lightning bolt struck, it was believed that this was because Veles hid from Perun under or behind that particular place. In the end, Perun managed to kill Veles, or to chase him back down into his watery underworld. The supreme god thus reestablished order in the world, which had been disrupted by his chaotic enemy. He then returned to the top of the World tree and proudly informed his opponent down in the roots "Well, there is your place, remain there!" This line comes from a Belarusian folk tale.

To the Slavs, the mythological symbolism of a supreme heavenly god who battles with his underworldly enemy through storms and thunder was extremely significant. While the exact pantheon characterizations differed between the various Slavic tribes, Perun is generally believed to have been considered as the supreme God by the majority, or perhaps by nearly all Slavs, at least towards the end of Slavic paganism. The earliest supreme God was probably Rod; it is unclear precisely how and why his worship as the head of the pantheon evolved into the worship of Perun."

And in those few words, we can see immediately both a solar and a seasonal aspect to this myth as well as even perhaps a tree of life? Interesting too that the underworld God Veles is symbolized by a dragon or serpent representing earth energies? Interesting also that his world is watery. Meanwhile, Perun is airy representing the sky and upper world, and fiery by virtue of the weapons at his disposal – so we have also the four elements. The story also hints at finding balance between the elements as does the hexagram. The hexagram is nothing but a representation of the four elements anyway. So, there is also an As above, So below here. You see, there is so much occult knowledge communicated in just this paraphrasing of the myth, one has to marvel at our ancestors.

Perun

How mighty thou art O' God of the skies

Endlessly chasing the horned God of lies

An immortal cycle of endings and beginnings

And this is the meaning of the World

It's the darkness stealing the fire at night

And the first glowing dawn of light

It's the creation of many

Tested in the fires

Some are destroyed

Others forged in steel

It is an ever-turning wheel

The cycle of life

And death

To begin

We must have an ending

And somewhere

There is balance

In the shifting sands of time

The fleeting balance

Of a line in creation

A crack of thunder

Now even before I really begin, I can see some really intriguing elements to these Slavic Gods. The symbol for Perun is a Hexagon, In their eternal battle, Perun is often shown on horseback lancing Veles who in turn is symbolized as a dragon or serpent. Now, where have I seen that image before?

So, in addition to exploring the land in search of earth energies in my adopted land, I am now wanting to explore Slavic myth, legend and fairy tale to try to understand how they – the Slavs who occupied this part of the world, saw the land that they had adopted when standing on the mountain north of Prague called Mount Říp. It was here that the three Slav brother, Čech, Lech and Mech, looked over the lands they would adopt and inhabit, so the myth says.

Several years ago, Sue Vincent and I wrote a book about the Hexagram[32]. The book explores that symbol. "*Not from some scholarly or deeply complex perspective but seeing it as a representation relating to life and living. The forces and pressures that are associated with the hexagram are, after all the forces of life at both practical and Universal levels. By exploring and beginning to understand the symbol, we are able to learn and discover more about ourselves.*" On the website for the book[33], I have occasionally written posts to show how the hexagram is a key of sorts to help unlock deeper mysteries in many different occult symbols or methods. In the last few months, as I explored the Czech landscape, the Slavic landscape to be more precise, I came across yet another example.

In Slavic myth as we saw above, the world is seen as a tree – a tree of life if you will. In fact, it may be that the ancient Slavs worshipped trees and the Gods associated with them. So imagine

---

[32] See Bibliography
[33] https://www.mystical-hexagram.com

87

from this Slavic perspective that creation is a tree – a huge and ancient Oak. The huge Oak reaches up to the sky and its branches reach up to heaven while its solid roots reach to the underworld. The trunk is the world. Now, atop the tree and the ruler of heaven is the mighty Perun, God of thunder and lightning and often symbolized by the Eagle and by storms. A mighty warrior wielding a mighty battle axe riding a chariot. His weapon is lightning or golden apples that he throws at his enemies. He is representative of Fire and Air. Beneath him, ruling the underworld is Veles, a trickster, a shapeshifter and symbolized by the serpent. He is often pictured as having the head of a bear and the body of a serpent, and he punishes with disease. Veles is representative of Earth and Water.

In the myth of the Slavic world tree, Perun and Veles are in constant battle. Veles comes up and steals Perun's cattle, wife or children. Perun chases Veles shooting lightening at him in the end killing Veles. Of course, Veles always comes back to life and the process is repeated. In fact, Perun is often shown as a figure on horseback spearing the dragon Veles – just like St., George or probably more closely – St. Michael.

Figure 15: 8th Century image of Perun defeating Veles

There are many levels to this myth obviously, but while one suggests the cycle of the year with winter and summer – light and dark, it is also a story of balance – the balance of the seasons, the balance of the cycles, life and death, and so on. It is also another version of the hexagram. As Perun is Fire (and Air) overlaying Veles' Earth (and Water). When placed one on top of the other – hey presto – you have a hexagram with its central point of balance.

Most recently, I learned of a Slavic Goddess named Živa or life. Somehow, I see Živa as important to me. Every day, as I walk the dog or myself around Špilberk Castle, I more and more felt as if I am very fortunate to live just underneath it. At least for now. When my own place is ready, I will move away from it and will need to find somewhere else to walk. I always feel liberated and rejuvenated up on the hill. It is often breezy, and the views of the city and surrounding countryside are stunning. Today was no exception.

A few weeks ago, though, I noticed for the first time that spring was arriving. Small blooms of orange, purple and white appeared as if overnight. It made one feel joyous somehow to see these small beautiful colorful flowers! Combined with the magnificent views, it made for an uplifting experience and once again, I felt that connection to the land and to Živa, and other aspects of the Goddess. Even the Moon – a half disk – was also visible. On one side of the Castle, the Sun was magnificent in the sky. He shone down on me, Rocky and Brno, peeking behind clouds. While on the other, the Moon reflected its light on us too.

We live in a world that is solar. It is black and white – a duality of ideologies. The harsh light of the Sun seems to be burning rather than sustaining – causing a dry, arid, and masculine heat. Meanwhile, the world of shades of grays and of reflection in which our emotional selves can be washed and cleaned has all but disappeared? I suspect much of this is an illusion – it is brought into an extreme 'light' by the brightness of the solar maleness.

For most of my adult life – certainly my magical life, I have sought out the goddess. I do not know why, but I have a sense of longing for the goddess. I have many images of goddesses scattered about my home. My inner contact identifies as female to me. The watery, earthy side of humanity has been not just been suppressed but often brutally deprived of any recognition. The dry wizened old men took the voluptuous and at times brazen Goddess and they put her in a habit. They boiled her down to Mary, Mother of God, subservient to them and deprived her of any sexuality at all. In a sense, it seems symbolic of modern life.

The Moon is reflective, and it goes through phases - back and forth – a set of shades of grey. Živa, is the water of life – the waters of the womb where it is warm and dark. This lunar aspect is the emotional side of our lives. I'm not advocating switching one extreme for the other, but I am seeking the balance in between. We don't need women trying to emulate men! We need women being women and bringing the feminine or lunar attributes to bear in all walks and levels of life. Men need to reconcile with their inner suppressed female side. We need to remember how to venerate the sacred feminine and bring the Goddess back into our daily lives. We need to see that things are shades of grey and that reflection is often better than either obsession or spotlighting. The cooling waters of reflection are needed to balance the burning sunlight of focus. We need to work on the emotional side of ourselves and not just on the 'betterment' of life the application of technology without consideration of its emotional and social impacts. It's time for the Goddess to make a re-entry into all of our lives – in all of Her aspects.

I suspect it is just around the corner – if not already happening. I feel Her approaching. I hear Her laughter. She is in the forests, flowing in the streams, the eternal Mother is returning. And She is needed. I realized too what it I love about this country – the Czech Republic – the Slavic east – It's that She is so close.

Chasing the Shaman

About a month after my encounter with the shaman near my apartment and as all of the above was going on, Tünde and I were walking down my street when she noticed something strange. She pointed it out to me, and we went over to look. It was what appeared to be a plate and a soup dish on top of that. Inside the soup dish was a stone and a cigar stub. It was the shaman! I told her, *"Look it is the cigar stub and the stone that gives it away."*

Figure 16: The Shaman's Mark

A day later, as I walked the dog, I revisited this location and discovered the dish and plate had gone and been replaced by a set of stones, metal rods and other items, to form what looked like an arrow. Around the stones in the middle were 2 or 3 hand rolled cigarette ends that had burned down leaving long ashes. I then walked a hundred meters or so to the site of the skeleton and here was also an arrangement laid out in pebbles also pointing in much the same direction. Once again, I was puzzled by this.

Now, each day, when I took the dog, I was visiting both sites and observing a constant rearrangement of stones and items. One day, there were Reindeer antlers and sticks involved and the next, they were gone. The arrow shapes changed each day and burned out cigarettes would be placed on top of one of the larger rocks. I was trying to catch him in the act to find out who he was, what he was doing and why? Yet, whenever I went there was evidence of him being there – different arrangement, added stones, or cigarettes or cigar butts, but no shaman.

Figure 17: The Arrow

A few days later, I discovered a third site nearby. Here, a single pebble was placed, and a cigar butt placed by its side. A few days went by and the pebble was gone only to show up in the main stone arrangement. I watched carefully and photographed all the evidence like a forensics expert. Desperate, I picked out my own pebble and placed it next to a new one he had placed in his stone charging location. The next day, he had moved my stone to sit beside his. I moved it back again. The next day, his stone had gone but mine remained. He must know I knew. His stone showed up in the stone arrangement.

Figure 18: One version of the Shaman's Arrow

consulted Sue. I consulted others. But no one seemed to know what he was up to except one Slavic shaman I wrote too told me that working with stones like this was an old practice and energy work – similar to standing stones, the stones and pebbles collected and redirected and amplified natural energies. She was amazed I had noticed and called it a mirror reality for me. A mirror reality? Interesting.

I soon also realized that his activity was tied to the Moon phases. He started a new design at a New Moon gradually building it until the Full Moon and then it would remain relatively unchanged until the next new moon when everything was structurally changed.

Figure 19: Another Version

For this lunar cycle, he has changed things again. Everything is now at the skeleton site and it is divided in two halves. Both sets of stones make an arrow and one points to the other and through the indentation made purposefully that had the pebble in it that I had accidentally kicked and replaced. One arrangement contains the larger rocks surrounded by pebbles in a circular arrangement while a short distance away, is another arrow shape made of smaller pebbles and rocks. A couple of days ago, I had to laugh when I saw he had also placed an old wooden toilet seat and cover at the head of the arrow arrangement! He is resourceful, this shaman.

would like to find him and talk with him. Perhaps the language barrier would be too great but by all accounts, this is a real shaman working in perhaps a Slavic tradition with energized stones. still do not know his intention but with the burned flowers and also the small and beautiful broach he had placed on the main rock for a few days, it does seem to involve the loss of someone. Perhaps he is helping them in the next world? Maybe I am totally wrong and these and his tobacco are simply offerings to the old Gods?

Figure 20: Another Version

think the key thing is that I noticed this activity. No one else seems to. It is a mirror reality perhaps caused by the fact that I am giving my attention to the earth energies in this country and earning how historically, people have approached, worked with and worshipped those energies. Perhaps Sue and Stuart are right. Maybe there is a karmic connection or a reincarnation aspect to all of this for me? Time will tell. Meanwhile, I am chasing the shaman daily.

What have I learned in all of this? Well, I have again tuned into the magic that happens when you follow a certain path. The negativity I had fallen into has largely gone and has been replaced by positivity about this country and even its people. My work has just begun here and there is much to do in terms of working with and mapping the energies here. I am excited to be doing just that and sharing these activities with my daughter, Tünde, my friends and you. It seems to me that I am back on whatever path I am supposed to be walking to a large degree – the magic shows me this. My record is playing, and I am listening. I am enjoying it and life has real meaning again.

And surely, in the end, that is what matters.

Živa

Packets of water

Jostle moving downstream

A rushing whine

Grabs my soul

As I tumble and roll away

Her hair envelopes

Like a curtain waterfall

The living waters

Suck me down

Cleansing, refreshing

She giggles and bubbles

And all of my struggles

Are washed away

Her caress

I must profess

Waters that coalesce

Exciting the senses

Emerging whole and cleansed

The Man

The Goddess

Blessed

About G. Michael Vasey

With over 40 books in print, Gary is an established author with notable contributions in the areas of the paranormal (including several #1 best sellers in the Supernatural category), metaphysics, poetry, and business. He is also a collector of strange stories at My Haunted Life Too. In 2016, he resumed his interest in music and released two albums of self-penned and self-performed songs that are available at all digital music stores. Since then, he has been churning out catchy songs at a rapid rate and captured the interest of a growing audience.

He was born in the city of Hull in England, and grew up in East Yorkshire, the eldest of three boys. Growing up can be extremely tough for any kid, but imagine growing up around poltergeist activity and ghosts? G. Michael Vasey had exactly that kind of childhood, experiencing ghosts, poltergeists, and other strange and scary, supernatural phenomena. In fact, he seemed to attract it, developing an interest in the occult and supernatural at an early age and he has been fascinated ever since.

His "My Haunted Life" trilogy has been highly successful–reaching number one on bestseller lists on both sides of the Atlantic. Now he is also presenting the stories of others. His book about the Black Eyed Kids is currently available on Amazon and continues to capture the morbid interest of hundreds of fans. It's a must-read for anyone with an interest in the strange happenings of the paranormal world.

Then there's "*The Pink Bus and Other Strange Stories from LaLa Land*," a book that lifts the veil on one of the biggest mysteries in human history–the process of death, and what happens to our souls when we die. His novella – The Last Observer – won critical praise and is a twisty story about the nature of reality and magic. His most recent books have included a tour of the supernatural side of the Czech Republic, a set of Kindle shorts on topics like Poltergeists, Ghosts of the Living (bilocation) and The BEK now issued as a compilation volume, a new book of poetry, a look at the recently headlining topic of paranormal sex and, the Halloween Vault of Horror, a new collection of true paranormal stories.

He has appeared on numerous radio shows such as

* Mysterious Radio,
* Jim Harold's paranormal podcasts,
* The Knight's Pub,
* True Ghost Stories Online and
* X Radio with Rob McConnell

He has also been featured in Chat – Its Fate magazine and been interviewed by Ghost Village and Novel Ideas, amongst others. He also contributed regularly to the Westerner magazine with his 'Paranormal Corner' feature.

Whether you've heard one of G. Michael Vasey's radio appearances, or read one of his books over the shoulders of an avid reader on the bus, or whether you've simply got an interest in the paranormal and stumbled upon this page… You are going to pulled into the paranormal world of G. Michael Vasey, and you will be hooked.

You can discover much more about the supernatural at www.gmichaelvasey.com or read true scary stories at www.myhauntedlifetoo.com.

'In many ways, I have been very fortunate meeting many wonderful people and visiting a great many beautiful and interesting places in my life to date. Some of my blog articles highlight these wonderful experiences…..In the end, I am fascinated by what we are and why we are here. I am captivated by reality and what it might be. I am a firm believer in magic and the power of the mind to shape reality. That's what I write about, think about, and obsess about….."

Gary has also studied magic for many years with organizations like AMORC, CR&C, SOL and The Silent Eye. He is a second degree initiate of SOL and performed as a supervisor for the school for many years. He has written several books on magic including The Mystical Hexagram penned with Sue Vincent and The New You.

Other Books

- **The Scary Best of My Haunted Life Too** (ebook)
- **Motel Hell** (ebook)
- **G. Michael Vasey's Halloween Vault of Horror** (ebook)
- **The Seduction of the Innocents** (ebook, audiobook and Paperback)
- **The Chilling, True Terror of the Black-Eyed Kids – A Compilation** (Paperback, Audiobook and ebook)
- **Poltergeist – The Noisy Ghosts** (ebook)
- **Ghosts of the Living** (ebook)
- **Your Haunted Lives 3 – The Black Eyed Kids** (ebook)
- **Lord of the Elements (The Last Observer 2)** (ebook and Paperback)
- **True Tales of Haunted Places** (ebook)
- **The Most Haunted Country in the World – The Czech Republic** (ebook, paperback, audiobook)
- **Your Haunted Lives – Revisited** (ebook and Audiobook)
- **The Pink Bus** (ebook and audio book)
- **Ghosts in The Machines** *(ebook and audiobook)*
- **The New You** *(Paperback, ebook and audiobook)*
- **God's Pretenders – Incredible Tales of Magic and Alchemy** *(ebook and audiobook)*
- **My Haunted Life – Extreme Edition** *(Paperback, audiobook and ebook)*
- **My Haunted Life 3** *(Audiobook and eBook)*
- **My Haunted Life Too** *(Audio book and ebook)*
- **My Haunted Life** *(ebook and audiobook)*
- **The Last Observer** *(Paperback, ebook and Audiobook)*
- **The Mystical Hexagram** *(Paperback and ebook)*
- **Inner Journeys – Explorations of the Soul** *(Paperback and ebook)*

Other Poetry Collections

- **Reflections on Life: Spiritual Poetry** (ebook and paperback)
- **The Dilemma of Fatherhood** (ebook)
- **Death on The Beach** *(ebook)*
- **The Art of Science** *(Paperback and ebook)*
- **Best Laid Plans and Other Strange Tails** *(Paperback and ebook)*
- **Moon Whispers** *(Paperback and ebook)*
- **Astral Messages** *(Paperback and ebook)*
- **Poems for the Little Room** *(Paperback and ebook)*
- **Weird Tales** *(Paperback and ebook)*

All of G. Michael's Vasey's books can be obtained from many retailers and book selling sites. He offers signed and dedicated paperbacks from his website at https://www.garymvasey.com

Bibliography

Bates, Brian. *The Way of Wyrd: Tales of an Anglo-Saxon Sorcerer*, 2004, Hay House UK

Broadhurst, Paul, *The Green Man and the Dragon, 2006,* Mythos Press

France, Stuart & Vincent , S.C. *The Initiate.* 2020, The Silent Eye Press (Originally published as *The Initiate: Adventures in Sacred Chromatography* by Sue Vincent and Stuart France, 2013

Le Guin, Ursula. The *Wizard of Earthsea*, 1968, Parnassus Press

Miller, Hamish & Broadhurst, Paul. *The Sun and The Serpent*, 1994, Pendragon Partnership

Parker, Posh. *Bus to Bohemia,* 2010, New Generation Publishing

Vasey, G. Michael, *The Czech Republic – The Most Haunted Country in the world*, 2016, Asteroth's Books

Vasey, G. Michael, *The New You: How to Create Your Own Reality*, 2nd Ed, 2015, Asteroth's Books

Vasey, G. Michael, 2013. The Last Observer: A Magical Battle for Reality, Roundfire Books

Vasey, G. Michael, 2005. *Inner Journeys: Explorations of the Soul.* Thoth Publications

Vasey, G. Michael & Vincent, S.C., The Mystical Hexagram: The Seven Inner Stars of Power, Ed. 2, 2015, Asteroth's Books

Printed in Great Britain
by Amazon